The Future of Anglicanism

The Future of Anglicanism

Edited by
Robert Hannaford

Gracewing.

First published in 1996

Gracewing
Fowler Wright Books
2 Southern Avenue, Leominster
Herefordshire HR6 0Q

UK ISBN 0 85244 349 8

Typesetting by Action Typesetting Ltd,
Gloucester, GL1 1SP

Printed by Cromwell Press,
Broughton Gifford, Wiltshire, SN12 8PH

Contents

Notes on Contributors

Paul Avis is an Anglican priest and theologian, operating from a group of rural parishes near Exeter, Devon. He is the author of many books and articles, including *Anglicanism and the Christian Church* (1989) and *Christians in Communion* (1990), and also serves as a member of the Church of England Doctrine Commission.

Timothy Bradshaw is an Anglican priest on the staff of Regents Park College, Oxford, where he is Tutor in Doctrine and Dean. The author of several books, including *The Olive Branch: An Evangelical Anglican Doctrine of the Church* (1992), he is also a member of the International Anglican-Orthodox Dialogue and on the English-Roman Catholic Committee.

Mark Chapman studied in Oxford and in Munich and is Lecturer in Systematic Theology at Ripon College Cuddesdon, Oxford and Non-Stipendiary priest in the Dorchester-on-Thames Team Ministry, Oxfordshire.

Peter Davie is Senior Lecturer in Religious Studies at Canterbury Christ Church College, where he teaches Church History. Prior to his present appointment he served as a full-time parish priest, and he now acts as an honorary assistant priest in the Canterbury City Centre Parish. He is the author of *Pastoral Care and the Parish* (1983).

Samuel L. Edwards is a priest of the Episcopal Church in the United States of America and Executive Director of the Episcopal Synod of America, Fort Worth, Texas.

Gillian R. Evans lectures in Theology and Church History in the University of Cambridge and was British Academy Research Reader in Theology (1986–8). She is a member of the Faith and Order Advisory Group of the Church of England's General Synod and the author of many books and articles including *Authority in the Church: a challenge for Anglicans* (1990) and *The Church and the churches* (1994).

John Halliburton is a Residentiary Canon of St Paul's Cathedral, London. Currently Chairman of the Church Union's Theological Committee he was for several years a member of the Church of England Doctrine Commission and acted as a consultant to the Anglican-Roman Catholic International Commission. A theologian and church historian, he is the author of a number of studies, including *The Authority of a Bishop* (1987).

Robert Hannaford is Senior Lecturer in Theology and Director of the Centre for the Study of Christianity at Canterbury Christ Church College and honorary assistant priest in the parish of Harbeldown, Canterbury. He has taught at Exeter and Oxford Universities and was formerly Tutor in Doctrine at St Stephen's House, Oxford. A specialist in Systematic and Philosophical Theology he has published several essays and papers on ecclesiology and Anglican Theology.

Kenneth A. Locke has studied theology at the School of Hebrew, Biblical and Theological Studies at Trinity College, Dublin since 1989. A native of the United States of America, he is currently working on a doctoral thesis which examines various aspects of Anglican ecclesiology.

Foreword

Issues such as the revision of the liturgy, the ordination of women to the episcopate and priesthood, inculturation, ecclesial authority in a pan-Anglican context and plurality and the bonds and limits of communion have brought to a head internal tensions that have their roots deep within Anglican history. Since its emergence in the nineteenth and twentieth centuries the Anglican communion of churches has experienced profound difficulties in defining itself. As William Sachs notes in a recent study of the development of Anglicanism, 'A cacophony of voices with equal claim to being normatively Anglican has arisen without a means to mediate among them'. As a result 'the history of modern Anglican life reveals a bewildering profusion of claims to be Anglican and a pervasive tension between order and community'.[1]

The root of the problem facing Anglicanism lies in the manifold ways in which Anglicans have sought 'a definitive way to be both grounded in diverse cultures and genuinely apostolic'.[2] Anglicanism is searching for a coherent theological rationale for its emergence as a global communion of churches. The claim sometimes made by Anglicans in England that their church is nothing more nor less than the catholic Church of the English nation with its bishops occupying the ancient sees cannot be easily transposed to other Anglican contexts. In this respect the English theologian A.E.J. Rawlinson was surely right when he sensed that the question of Anglican coherence and identity only emerged with full force once Anglicanism was compelled to think of itself not merely in relation to the English but to humankind as a whole.[3] Once Anglicanism ceased to be merely a phenomenon of the British Empire and the English Diaspora, an element of ecclesial re-identification was inevitable. What had for a brief time been defined as the catholic and reformed faith of the English people was now forced by circumstances to think of itself as Anglicanism, a faith for people of any and all nations.

The papers in this book are offered as a constructive and scholarly contribution to the ongoing discussion of Anglican faith and order. Drawn from the various traditions within Anglicanism – catholic, liberal and evangelical – the contributors utilise the resources of historical, biblical and theological scholarship to examine various aspects of Anglican tradition and practice, assess the state of contemporary Anglicanism and raise questions about its future direction. Paul Avis opens the discussion by questioning the tendency of Anglicans to stress the provisionality of their church. He insists that a future for Anglicanism depends upon a confident and robust grasp of the Anglican way of being Christian. Tim Bradshaw and Samuel Edwards are less sanguine about the future. Bradshaw argues that contemporary Anglicanism, particularly in England, has been too quick to assimilate its traditional faith to the mores of secular culture and invites us to recover its Christological centre. Writing from the American context, Samuel Edwards contemplates the dissolution of Christendom and describes the present age as a time of convergence and realignment in world Christianity. He invites Anglicans, particularly those in the catholic and evangelical traditions, to grasp the moment as an opportunity for growth and renewal. Mark Chapman, Kenneth Locke and Peter Davie each address aspects of the history of Anglicanism that have major implications for its future direction. Mark Chapman examines the Anglican appropriation of Cyprianic ecclesiology and finds in it an important theological resource for the doctrine of provincial autonomy. Kenneth Locke provides a critical discussion of the Anglican Newman's appeal to antiquity as a guide to orthodoxy in matters of faith while Peter Davie examines the rise of a distinctively Anglican approach to pastoral theology, attuned to both traditional faith and the developments of modern science and learning, in the late Victorian Church of England. Finally, Gillian Evans, John Halliburton and Robert Hannaford respond positively to the debate within Anglicanism following the admission of women to the episcopate and priesthood. In her essay Gillian Evans warns against the dangers of party-spirit and examines the background to the discussion of conciliar authority within the Anglican communion. John Halliburton discusses the central role of the episcopate within catholic Christianity and points to the need for clarity and definition in the discussion of doctrinal differences. The question of communion has become a vital concern to contemporary Anglicans. In his paper Robert Hannaford sets out to uncover the ecclesiology of communion and concludes by considering the current Anglican predicament.

The papers in this book originated in two major international conferences held at Canterbury Christ Church College in 1994 and

1995. The first dealt with the *Future of Anglicanism* and was held under the aegis of the college's department of Religious Studies and its Centre for the Study of Christianity. The second was the third meeting of the International (Anglican) Bishops' Conference on Faith and Order and addressed the subject of *Authority, Order and Communion* within Anglicanism. The editor wishes to acknowledge the support of Canterbury Christ Church College for sponsoring the first conference and facilitating the production of this volume, and that of the Church Union for making the second conference possible.

The Presentation of the Lord
1996

Notes

1. W. Sachs, *The Transformation of Anglicanism: From State Church to Global Communion* (CUP, Cambridge/New York, 1993), p. 4.
2. ibid.
3. A.E.J. Rawlinson, *The Church of England and the Church of Christ* (Longmans, Green & Co., London, 1930), p. 4, 31, 77 & 88.

Keeping Faith with Anglicanism

Paul Avis

Two friends of mine were visiting the United States on business. They were entertained with typical American hospitality in the home of a customer. On Sunday morning their hosts explained that they usually went to church. Would their guests care to join them? Yes, they replied, they went to church too. 'We're Episcopalians,' the host family explained, 'how about you?' 'Oh, we're Church of England,' they replied. 'That's all right,' was the response, 'we may be different religions, but I guess we both worship the same God.' Clearly neither party had heard of the Anglican Communion – that world-wide fellowship of autonomous churches which share a broad tradition of theology, worship and spirituality, and have a common focus in the office of the Archbishop of Canterbury.

The casual attitude towards the Anglican Communion is not confined to some lay people. It also exists at an official level. A lack of seriousness about the Anglican tradition and Anglican ecclesiology has bedevilled our theological education and ecumenical involvement. I sometimes wonder whether Anglicans have faith in Anglicanism and whether they really want a future for the Anglican Communion. There are many challenges to the future of the Anglican Communion – particularly the issue of inculturation, with its threat to the coherent identity of the Anglican tradition in theology and liturgy, and the issue of authority and provincial autonomy, which has been intensified recently by the question of women priests and bishops. But the most radical challenge to the future of Anglicanism is expressed in the question: 'Do Anglicans really want a future for Anglicanism?'

The Provisionality of Anglicanism

Anglican spokesmen (and they have consistently been spokes*men*) have long adopted the strange habit of talking down the future of

1

Anglicanism. They have stressed its provisional nature and spoken of its need to find itself assimilated into the wider Church. They seem to have difficulty in finding a rationale for the existence of Anglicanism. The tendency is not confined to the Church of England. The American, Bishop Stephen Bayne, the first executive officer of the Anglican Communion, claimed forty years ago:

> The vocation of Anglicanism is, ultimately, to disappear. That is its vocation precisely because Anglicanism does not believe in itself but it believes only in the Catholic Church of Christ; therefore it is for ever restless until it finds a place in that body.[1]

I must confess that I find this statement – recently endorsed in a report of the Church of England's General Synod – rather disturbing. What Stephen Bayne asserts of the Anglican Communion is no more and no less true of the Anglican Communion than it is of any part of the Church Catholic.

The Catholic Church that we confess in the Creed is not an empirical entity: it cannot be located geographically and it is not sociologically identifiable. I say this, not because I think that the Catholic Church is an invisible, ethereal and intangible entity, that cannot come down to earth – on the contrary, the Catholic Church is thoroughly incarnational and is by its nature a visible society – but because the Christian Church in the world is divided and fragmented. Its participation in catholicity is partial and incomplete. It can only aspire to a catholicity that remains ultimately eschatological – that is to say, it will be fulfilled when God's plan of salvation is perfected beyond this life. All parts of the Christian Church, large and small, not just Anglicanism, stand in this position of incompleteness and fragmentation *vis-à-vis* the Catholic Church of the Creed. There is no already existing 'body', as Bayne puts it, within which Anglicanism seeks a home.

According to Bayne, Anglicanism does not believe in itself but only in the Catholic Church. But what is unique to Anglicanism in that? I trust that no branch of the Christian Church believes in itself rather than in the Catholic Church of Christ. But that trust is called into question when some great communions – namely the Roman Catholic Church and the Orthodox Churches – tend to identify their empirical communions with the Church of Christ *tout court*. Both Rome and the Orthodox have traditionally held that their churches are identical with the Catholic Church, without remainder. Thankfully, in Rome since Vatican II and among the Orthodox also, there are the beginnings of a relativisation of these absolutist claims.

As is well known, the Second Vatican Council, in its Constitution on the Church (*Lumen Gentium*), used the subtle phrase 'subsists in' for the relationship between the Roman Catholic Church and the Church of Christ. This enabled the Council to give a degree of recognition – albeit muted and qualified – to ecclesial bodies outside the Roman Catholic Church.

> The unique Church of Christ which in the Creed we avow as one, holy, catholic and apostolic ... constituted and organised in the world as a society, subsists in the Catholic Church, which is governed by the successor of Peter and by the bishops in union with that successor, although many elements of sanctification and of truth can be found outside of her visible structure. These elements, however, as gifts properly belonging to the Church of Christ, possess an inner dynamism toward Catholic unity.[2]

Since Vatican II, the phrase 'subsists in' has continued to intrigue and perplex interpreters. It is not part of our task here to pin down the meaning of this elusive and wonderfully nuanced expression. It obviously needs to be understood in conjunction with the Constitution on Ecumenism, which in fact further relativises traditional Roman claims. Suffice it to say that it clearly rules out any assertion that the Roman Catholic Church is to be identified with the Church of Christ entirely and without remainder.

The Anglican-Roman Catholic International Commission (ARCIC) correctly states that 'the Second Vatican Council, while teaching that the Church of God subsists in the Roman Catholic Church, rejected the position that the Church of God is co-extensive with the Roman Catholic Church and is exclusively embodied in that Church'. However, I have reservations about the conclusion that ARCIC derives from this. It goes on to say that Vatican II 'allows it to be said that a church out of communion with the Roman see may lack nothing from the viewpoint of the Roman Catholic Church except that it does not belong to the visible manifestation of full Christian communion which is maintained in the Roman Catholic Church'. In a sense this is true: ecclesial communities (Vatican II is equivocal about calling them Churches) separated from Rome possess all the attributes of Church life that they can possess in separation. That is merely a truism. In the Roman Catholic understanding, those attributes do not include 'fullness of unity', the sacrament of orders, and 'the genuine and total reality of the Eucharistic mystery'. Those are not trivial omissions from what Vatican II allows to churches not in communion with Rome![3]

Similarly, there are voices among the Orthodox who are asking: Granted that the unchanging teaching and tradition of our Church is that the Orthodox Churches do indeed constitute the Church of Christ, what does this imply for our assessment of other ecclesial bodies? Does it require us to say that they are nothing, and if it does not require us to say that, what are they? How should we evaluate the theological status of the ecclesial reality that they evidently possess? As participants in the Faith and Order movement since 1927 and as founder members of the World Council of Churches (1948), the Orthodox could hardly avoid this question, but it seems to have been intensified for them by recent ecumenical dialogue.[4]

While these two great communions are beginning to moderate their traditional exclusive claims, Anglicans have never officially made any such claim. Since Richard Hooker at the end of the sixteenth century, they have acknowledged that they are merely a part, portion or branch of the whole catholic Church. Thus Anglicans can do what no true died-in-the-wool Roman Catholic or Orthodox can do, and that is to place Rome and the Orthodox, together with Lutherans, Reformed, Methodists, Old Catholics, and all others who have an ecclesiology of the Church as a visible society transcending the local congregation and exerting a degree of authority over it, on the same footing with his or her own Anglican Church, as fragments of the whole, acknowledging that all are victims of disunity, all share in the responsibility for schism, and all are called to work for the healing of the wounds of the body of Christ. (That does not imply that there are not degrees of participation in the unity, catholicity and apostolicity of the Church – but that is another subject.)

When Archbishop Robert Runcie formally opened the 1988 Lambeth Conference, welcoming the bishops of the Anglican Communion who had responded to his invitation, he rightly stressed that 'we must never make the survival of the Anglican Communion an end in itself'. He correctly explained that 'the Churches of the Anglican Communion have never claimed to be more than a part of the One, Holy, Catholic and Apostolic Church'. Archbishop Runcie then went on, however, to make the further statement that 'Anglicanism has a radically provisional character which we must never allow to be obscured'.[5] How should we interpret this assertion about the provisionality of Anglicanism?

If Dr Runcie meant that the Anglican Communion, *like all communions of the Christian Church,* is partial and incomplete, and is impoverished by not being in full communion with its sister churches, and *like all communions of the Christian Church*, is highly provisional in relation to the eschatologically perfectly Church of the Creed, then his statement commands our wholehearted assent. If, however, he was implying that Anglicanism is peculiarly provisional, that it is somehow more provisional than other branches of the Christian Church, that it is Anglicanism's *forte*, so to speak, to be provisional in a way that other churches are not provisional, then I would feel bound to demur. In fact I would feel bound to say that, if that is what is meant, it is not only mistaken, but positively unhelpful.

Our great need at the present time as Anglicans, I believe, is to have confidence in our Anglican ecclesiology, our Anglican tradition and our Anglican Communion. We need the assurance that Anglicanism is an estimable manifestation of the Christian Church, that it has all the resources, by the grace of God, to meet the pastoral and spiritual needs of its members, that it has the authority to call to its ministry those whom it believes the Holy Spirit is calling and to bestow on them the authority of the Church that is catholic and apostolic, and, moreover, that it has much to offer the larger Church, the greater communion, for which we hope and work and pray. The Canons of the Church of England claim that for the Anglican Church in England when they affirm that it 'belongs to the true and apostolic Church of Christ' and go on to insist that 'no member thereof shall be at liberty to maintain or hold the contrary' (Canon A1). All Anglicans surely need to be convinced, with regard to their own church, of the truth of what this canon affirms with regard to the Church of England.

Parish clergy need the assurance that they are part of an institution that is worth its salt, if they are to give of their best. It is not helpful to tell them that the church that has called, trained and ordained them is provisional. If we want to evoke loyalty to the common cause, if we want to avoid producing alienated parochial clergy who are disillusioned with the institutional church, if we want to encourage the clergy to participate willingly in ministerial assessment and development programmes, then we must help them to believe in their church. We should, from time, to time and with a good conscience, celebrate its achievements under God through the centuries.

Bishops need this loyalty to the worth of Anglicanism and a due sense of the authority and integrity of the whole Anglican body – its conciliar nature – to protect them from their besetting sin, which is to become mere benevolent pragmatists, who decide policy (in so far as it is left by default in their hands) by measuring the competing pressures upon them rather than by reference to proven principles of Anglican ecclesiology. Our bishops need this assurance as those who are particularly called to be stewards of a tradition and teachers of the faith.

Lay people also need to be thoroughly convinced of the abiding value of Anglicanism when, as now, they are being asked to work harder, to give more generously, and to take on greater responsibilities. Motivation comes when they have the assurance that all this is for the sake of the church they love, a church that is worthy of the sacrifices that they are being asked to make. Such a church is not appropriately designated 'provisional'.

Finally, theologians need faith in their Anglican tradition to prevent them becoming irresponsibly eclectic, freelance theological pundits, but instead to practise what Karl Rahner calls 'theology in the bosom of the Church'. Our representatives who take part in bilateral ecumenical dialogues need this sense of assurance that there is a definite and distinct Anglican ecclesiology, that is of permanent validity for Anglicans. All these theologians will only have it if they have a sense of gratitude to their communion and if they feel nourished by its tradition of theology and liturgy. They will only have it too if they are steeped in the writings of the great formative theologians of Anglicanism, among whom Richard Hooker is by common consent supreme.

Having entered that important caveat against careless talk about the provisionality of Anglicanism, I am now, I hope, in a position to speak much more positively about the true provisionality of each and every one of the plurality of Christian churches that exists. But I want to be clear that the provisionality of the churches is a theological, not a sociological judgement. It is not related to their respective numbers, their relative antiquity or their diverse cultural character. As Duquoc puts it in his book *Provisional Churches*, 'the claim that the churches are provisional does not arise so much out of a purely sociological analysis of the variations between them, as out of a quest for their mystical or eschatological goal'.[6] Duquoc explains that

> The provisional denotes the fact that the churches are historical and therefore mortal; it is not a pejorative judgement, suggesting a lack of value... The provisional denotes the condition of innovation, of continual creation, of presence in changing situations: it is opposed to a stubborn concern to stop the moment, the mobility of forms or the mortality of relationships.[7]

A recent manifesto from the Groupe des Dombes (a seminar of French Protestants and Catholics that has met annually at the Cistercian Abbey of Les Dombes near Lyon since 1937 and has often set the pace for ecumenical progress) has some helpful things to say about provisionality. *For the Conversion of the Churches*[8] examines the concepts of identity and conversion in the Church. It distinguishes three levels of identity and conversion.

First, there is our basic *Christian* identity, the orientation of personal faith to Jesus Christ. Clearly this demands continual conversion to God.

Second, there is *ecclesial* identity, our fundamental belonging to the Christian Church. This calls for continual conversion to conform to the nature of the Church of Jesus Christ.

Finally, there is *confessional* identity, the historically constructed self-understanding that each church has evolved over against other churches. Conversion in this dimension requires that all churches recognise that they are confessional bodies, so relativising themselves *vis-à-vis* the one Church of Christ. For 'no confessional church can be identified as it stands with the Church of Jesus Christ'.

The Groupe des Dombes makes a useful distinction between 'confessional identity', which is the healthy recognition that one belongs to an historical church – and which is an essential prerequisite of any meaningful ecumenical dialogue – and 'confessionalism', which is a hardening of confessional identity into a defensive attitude of self-justification. Divisive confessional stances call for radical conversion of confessional identity. Because confessional identity has been created through separation, polemics and anathemas, it lacks ecclesial integrity and requires this integrity to be made up by continual conversion to God and the Church of God.

It is a remarkable insight of the document that it points out that the strength and distinctiveness of a church's confessional identity is also the source of its greatest temptation. For Protestants, it is suggested, the strength of their confessional identity lies in spontaneous obedience to the gospel, but the weakness springs from lack of attention to structures of visible continuity. For Catholics, the strength of their confessional identity is found in their grasp of the Church as a visible society, but the weakness arises from the tendency to try to construct institutional guarantees at the expense of the freedom of the Spirit. (Regrettably, the Group did not address the question of the strengths and weaknesses of Anglican confessional identity, but I shall say something about that shortly.) In fact, as the ecumenical dialogues show, Protestant churches are already sensitive to the need to provide for visible continuity, particularly in the form of the historic three-fold ministry. The Roman Catholic Church is here challenged to accept that it is a confessional church, like every other. It is called to conversion to the one Church of Jesus Christ. It needs to seek healing and fullness through communion with other churches.

For the Conversion of the Churches helps us to see a way in which
we can affirm an authentic confessional identity for Anglicanism
whilst at the same time acknowledging the provisionality of this identity through continual conversion to God who is the ultimate source
of the Church and the judge of all the separated churches.

Anglican Confessional Identity

Let us now turn to the question of Anglican confessional identity in
the restricted and provisional sense in which we are happy to allow
the use of this term. What is the content of Anglican confessional
identity? What are the spirit and forms of Anglicanism? What exactly
is this estimable expression of the Christian Church that we call
Anglicanism? The Lambeth Conference of 1930 defined the Anglican
Communion in a way that still seems helpful.[9] It stated the essential
Anglican position thus:

> The Anglican Communion is a fellowship, within the one, holy,
> catholic and apostolic Church, of those duly constituted dioceses,
> provinces, or regional Churches in communion with the see of
> Canterbury, which have the following characteristics in common:
>
> (a) they uphold and propagate the catholic and apostolic faith and
>   order as they are generally set forth in the Book of Common
>   Prayer as authorised in their several churches;
> (b) they are particular or national Churches, and as such, promote
>   within each of their territories a national expression of
>   Christian faith, life and worship; and
> (c) they are bound together not by a central legislative and exec-
>   utive authority but by mutual loyalty sustained by the common
>   counsel of the bishops in conference.

This definition, which carries the authority of the Lambeth
Conference, suggests several aspects of the Anglican Communion that
are worth underlining:

(1) It is not fortuitous that the Anglican Communion is a *commu-
      nion*. Its shared experience is one of fellowship. By adopting
      from the beginning the designation of a communion,
      Anglicanism seems particularly well placed to understand and
      contribute to the current quickening of interest in *koinonia*
      within ecumenical theology.
(2) The Anglican Communion belongs to the Christian Church.
      Its ecclesiology is founded on the principle that there is more

than one church that is catholic; that there are, therefore, non-Roman churches that are catholic; and that the existence of the Anglican Communion – far from being a denial of the credal doctrine of the unity, catholicity and apostolicity of the Church – is actually an instantiation of it.

(3) The faith and order of the Anglican Communion are held to be those that are characteristic of the Christian Church. They are set out in certain authoritative formularies, particularly the Book of Common Prayer (which is probably intended here to include the Thirty-Nine Articles and the Ordinal). It is acknowledged that the Book of Common Prayer has been both accepted and adapted throughout the Communion.

(4) Anglicanism acknowledges a providential ordering of distinct cultures and national destinies within which this common faith and order are expressed. The Anglican Communion is not about centralisation, uniformity or least of all Western imperialism and colonialism (that was a fact of history but essential Anglicanism is distinguishable from it). On the contrary, a principle of inculturation resides at the heart of the Anglican approach – however slow and reluctant Anglicans may have been to implement it in practice.

(5) The Anglican Communion has a common focus in the office of the Archbishop of the most ancient metropolitan see. The practical test of membership is being in communion with the Archbishop of Canterbury.

(6) However, neither the Archbishop of Canterbury nor the Lambeth Conference is given the authority to rule the Communion. The common counsel of bishops meeting in the Lambeth Conference guides the life of the Communion. Its bonds are therefore those of mutual loyalty and committed fellowship.

I would want to add one more characteristic of the Anglican Communion to those given by the Lambeth Conference of 1930. The *conciliar* nature of Anglicanism is certainly implicit in the Lambeth 1930 statement, but is not made explicit either there or in most discussions of Anglicanism. The Anglican Communion, with its Lambeth Conferences, its Anglican Consultative Council, its Primates' Meeting and its structures of synodical government at local, diocesan, and provincial or national levels, is an admirable example of conciliarity. It perpetuates the conciliar ideal as it was developed in the two centuries immediately preceding the Reformation at a time when the Western Church was disfigured by corruption and fragmented by division within the papacy itself. The conciliar movement aimed to reform the Church, expunge heresy and unite the papacy by calling together bishops, lay rulers and theologians in a free General Council that would ultimately be above the pope. Representative government was its guiding principle. The monarchical form of the papacy was its antagonist. Its triumph was the Council of Constance 1414-17. Though the conciliar movement was out-manoeuvred by the pope at the Council of Basel, its ideals continued to inspire reforming movements and were appealed to by both the continental and the English Reformers in the following century.

These ideals have come to fruition in modern Anglicanism. Though Anglicanism lacks a pope and denies the infallibility of councils, it implements the conciliar principle of representative government in which all estates of the Church can make their voices heard and in which the bishops remain the guardians of doctrine and worship. The synodical system is often criticised; in particular it is accused of aping parliamentary democracy. I cannot see anything to be ashamed of in that! But what its critics seem largely unaware of is the fact that the rationale for conciliar government stems from the pre-Reformation Church, that it was ecclesiologists and canon lawyers who argued the case for representative government, and that, if anything, it is parliament that has copied the conciliar procedures of the Christian Church. Ecclesiastical and secular forms of representative government developed in dialogue. There are many observers of Anglicanism, in more authoritarian and less tolerant churches, who would give their eye teeth to be allowed to debate freely the sort of theological issues that our synods have debated in recent years.

Let us now take a closer look at the distinctive faith and order of Anglicanism, which the Lambeth Conference of 1930 claimed was catholic and apostolic. Here I must ask my readers in the Anglican Communion at large for their understanding if I illustrate these mainly from the formularies of the Church of England, as the formularies best known to me. In the case of the Book of Common Prayer together with the Thirty-Nine Articles and the Ordinal, these historic formularies of the Church of England tend to have a special position in world Anglicanism as a paradigm of faith and order (as Lambeth 1930 recognised). I begin with some comments on Anglican faith.

Anglican Faith

Our starting point in considering Anglican faith might well be the Preface to the Declaration of Assent (Canon C15) which is read whenever bishops, priests or deacons are admitted to their ministry in the

Church of England (a number of other churches of the Anglican Communion have a similar statement). I choose this not because I regard it as definitive for the Anglican Communion, but as a convenient and succinct account of Anglican confessional identity.

> The Church of England [we can substitute here the name of our own Anglican Church] is part of the One, Holy, Catholic and Apostolic Church worshipping the one true God, Father, Son and Holy Spirit. It professes the faith uniquely revealed in the Holy Scriptures and set forth in the catholic creeds, which faith the Church is called upon to proclaim afresh in each generation. Led by the Holy Spirit, it has borne witness to Christian truth in its historic formularies, the Thirty-nine Articles of Religion, the Book of Common Prayer, and the Ordering of Bishops, Priests and Deacons.

I will make several observations on this statement.

(1) First and foremost, Anglicans insist that their churches belong to the one Church of Christ that we affirm in the creeds. As I have already mentioned, the Church of England's canons make it illegal for any member (in practice, any clerical member) to deny this. But putting the matter in this way – by using the term 'part' (The Episcopal Church of the USA uses 'portion' in the Preface to its Ordination Rites) – Anglicans show that they do not unchurch other communions or pass judgement on their ministries. It is not a function of Anglican self-definition to assert that Anglicanism alone constitutes the Church of Christ. Rather it is implicit in Anglican self-definition to allow that other churches also are parts or portions of the Church of Christ. This surely places an ecumenical perspective at the heart of Anglican ecclesiology.

(2) Anglicans take their stand, where their faith is concerned, on the unity and trinitarian identity of God, disclosed to us as Father, Son and Holy Spirit. Though there is more on the doctrine of the Trinity in the Thirty-Nine Articles, neither there nor here is there any speculative theology of the godhead. There is affirmation, but not speculation.

(3) This faith is said to be 'uniquely revealed' in the holy scriptures. Here the scriptures are accorded the status of the vehicle of revelation. But neither here nor in the Articles is there any theory of revelation or of biblical inspiration. The Articles state that 'Holy Scripture containeth all things necessary to salvation' and this is echoed in the Chicago-Lambeth Quadrilateral (1886-

88) which upholds the scriptures as 'the rule and ultimate standard of faith'. Anglican formularies do not recognise the
scriptures as a source of binding precepts and precedents which
should determine the worship or polity of the Church. Reason
and tradition also have their part to play.

(4)   The faith that is revealed in the scriptures is also 'set forth' in
the creeds that are received by the whole Church, that is, the
Apostles' Creed and the Niceno-Constantinopolitan Creed,
which are recited at the daily office and at the eucharist respec-
tively. There is a significant distinction between the function of
scripture which is to reveal and the function of the creeds which
is to 'set forth', that is to say, to manifest, exemplify or expose.
The Articles commend the creeds on the grounds that 'they may
be proved by most certain warrants of Holy Scripture.' The
Articles do not discuss the teaching status of the Fathers, though
they invoke Jerome and Augustine of Hippo in their support.
But the defenders of the English Reformation, such as John
Jewel, took their stand on scripture and the primitive Church.
The canons of the Church of England claim that its doctrine is
'grounded in the Holy Scriptures, and in such teachings of the
ancient Fathers and Councils of the Church as are agreeable to
the said Scriptures' (Canon A5).

(5)   It belongs, furthermore, to the Church's calling to proclaim
this faith – and not just to proclaim it, but to proclaim it afresh
in each generation. This seems to be a mandate for reinter-
pretation, re-expression and making the faith relevant –
provided, of course, that this exercise, necessary as it is,
remains essentially faithful to the scriptures and the creeds. I
note with pleasure that the Ordination of a Bishop in the
Episcopal Church of the USA calls upon him or her to
'proclaim and interpret the Gospel of Christ'.

(6)   Furthermore, Anglicans believe that they have been led by the
Holy Spirit to 'bear witness' to Christian truth in their historic
formularies. They do not claim to have plumbed the depths of
Christian truth, or to have exhaustively stated it, but to have
genuinely witnessed to or testified to it. I detect here a further
gradation in the claims that are being made. These formularies are not being placed on a par with scripture or the creeds.
Christian truth is said to be revealed in scripture, set forth in
the creeds, proclaimed by the Church, and witnessed to in the
formularies. I must confess that I find that a very satisfying
set of distinctions.

I have been quoting from the Church of England's Preface to the

Declaration of Assent. After the reading of this Preface, the candidates for the orders of bishop, priest or deacon make the Declaration of Assent. They are required to affirm their loyalty to this inheritance of faith as their inspiration and guidance under God in bringing the truth of Christ to their generation and in making him known to those in their care. These words will repay our closer study.

First, we notice that the truth that is drawn from scripture, the creeds and the historic formularies is described as an 'inheritance of faith'. This seems an apt expression: it implies something substantial and valuable coming down to us from the past, from our history, something that we thankfully receive, yet with a sense that there remains something for us to do in making it our own.

Second, what is demanded of us in relation to this inheritance is 'loyalty'. Now loyalty is a moral quality and an expression of character. It is the product of ethical nurture and disciplined obedience to the truth. Our response to the inheritance of faith is thus evoked in a personalist mode. It is something rather different from unquestioning submission to a dogma.

Third, this inheritance serves to provide 'inspiration and guidance'. This is, again, a very different matter from subscribing passively to dogma or blindly obeying a set of rules. Inspiration and guidance, like loyalty, belong to the realm of the moral and spiritual quest.

Altogether, the nuances in the Preface and the Declaration seem to give considerable scope for interpretation and exploration, provided that our fundamental loyalty to the inheritance of scripture, creeds and historic formularies is not eroded. The ideal here expressed seems to call for some such phrase as 'dynamic orthodoxy', where equal weight is placed on both halves of the equation. This concept represents an orthodoxy of intention, schooled in the inheritance of faith, yet open to new understandings in the light of the context within which the faith is to be proclaimed and applied; an orthodoxy that is not static, or lifeless, or merely reiterated again and again, regardless of whether anyone is listening, but one that is full of vitality and movement and has the flexibility to make contact with the diverse contexts of our pluralistic world.

Anglican Order

Now let us consider, more briefly, Anglican confessional identity as it is expressed in the Anglican understanding of church order – that is to say, the structures of ministry and government, the polity, of Anglicanism. Once again we find that what is claimed is intentionally limited and that there is a remarkable restraint in statements of Anglican order. The Lambeth Quadrilateral spoke simply of 'the historic episcopate, locally adapted in the methods of its administration to the varying needs of the nations and peoples called of God into the unity of his Church'. There is no theory here of why the historic episcopate is needed and no judgement on churches that lack it. There is no suggestion that it might be invalidated by a temporary break in the sequence of transmitted authority, nor is there any blueprint for a uniform model of episcopal structure. Adaptation to local needs is of the essence. As Louis Weil has well said, the episcopate emerged in the late sixteenth century as a fundamental characteristic of the Anglican understanding of the Church. Yet subsequent Anglican reflection on the episcopate has not defined the nature of that ministry in sharply exclusive terms. For, in Anglicanism, 'what is distinctive is not necessarily divisive'.[10]

The canons of the Church of England make a curiously minimalist claim for the Ordinal, asserting only that it 'is not repugnant to the Word of God' (Canon A4). But that does not mean that the Church of England (in this case) has any doubts about its authority to ordain or about the validity of the orders of those duly ordained by this instrument. On the contrary, it insists, in words that have a particular topical relevance in the light of current disagreements about the ordination of women, that they are lawfully ordained 'and ought to be accounted, both by themselves and others, to be truly bishops, priests or deacons'.

The 1662 Ordinal was confident that the threefold ministry went back to the apostles themselves. But the Alternative Service Book 1980 – reflecting the fact that biblical and patristic studies since the seventeenth century have shown the situation in the early Church to have been much more fluid and confused than was supposed then – contents itself with the attenuated statement: 'The Church of England maintains the historic threefold ministry of bishops, priests and deacons'. The only justification or rationale for the threefold ministry that is implied here is that it is 'historic'. This seems excessively minimalist and reductionist even for Anglicans!

The 1979 Book of Common Prayer of the Episcopal Church of the USA makes a stronger claim, observing that 'from the Apostles' time, there have been different ministries within the Church,' and claiming that the threefold order dates from 'the time of the New Testament'. The Prayer Book of the Church in Wales rather cannily refers the origins of the threefold ministry to a point somewhere in the first two centuries!

On this matter, Anglican practice is actually stronger than Anglican theory. The Book of Common Prayer 1662 states that no man shall be suffered to exercise any diaconal, priestly or episcopal function in the Church of England without episcopal ordination, and the American Prayer Book of 1979 lays it down that no one may exercise those three offices unless they have been ordained 'with the laying on of hands by bishops who are themselves duly qualified to confer Holy Orders'. But the Alternative Service Book 1980 of the Church of England calmly states that ministers of that church 'are ordained by bishops according to authorized forms of service, with prayer and the laying on of hands.'

Why have Anglicans consistently insisted on episcopal ordination since 1662? Whatever theological motives we may attribute to individual Anglican divines, I am convinced that Anglicans generally have held to episcopal ordination in historic succession because they have regarded it as an aspect of the catholicity and apostolicity of the Church. It is an aspect of Anglican ecclesiology that Anglicans share with the major historic communions of the Christian Church – the Roman Catholic, Orthodox, Oriental Orthodox, Old Catholic, and Nordic and Baltic Lutheran Churches. It does not imply an adverse judgement on the ministries of other churches, but remains a firm internal requirement of Anglicanism and part of its distinctive polity. Anglicans believe that it is integral to the apostolicity and catholicity of their church and it appears to follow that it should not be negotiable or compromised in ecumenical diplomacy.

Affirmation and Restraint

I discern in the Anglican tradition – and find inscribed in its formularies – a refreshing combination of two principles: affirmation and restraint. It is these two qualities, not in isolation or separation but in combination and interaction, that, I suggest, are typically Anglican. They infuse the confessional identity of Anglicanism, in the realms of both faith and order.

In the sphere of Anglican faith, the historic formularies are not claimed to be the last word in systematic theology, but are said to be 'agreeable to the Word of God'. The central truths of the Christian faith are roundly affirmed, but without going beyond what is revealed. It is a practical, not a speculative faith. Anglicans are invited to rehearse their faith primarily in liturgical and doxological form. Clergy are required to adhere to tradition through loyalty, respect and gratitude, rather than through juridical intimidation.

In the sphere of order, Anglicanism maintains the sufficiency of its ministries and sacraments. Their justification is not that they rest on some God-given guarantee, but that they are ministries and sacraments of the Church of Christ – and that is enough. The historic threefold ministry is upheld in a beautifully downbeat phrase as 'not repugnant to the Word of God', and no theory of this ministry is countenanced that would unchurch other bodies. It is a practical, not a speculative order, one attuned to pastoral care rather than to maintaining a hierarchical and authoritarian structure of doctrine and discipline.

Anglican faith and order are clearly central to Anglican confessional identity, in the sense of confessional identity – carefully distinguished from 'confessionalism' – worked out in the helpful recent publication of the Groupe des Dombes *For the Conversion of the Churches*. I have been suggesting that the faith and order of Anglicanism is marked by a combination and balance of affirmation and restraint. In their exercise of restraint, the seminal Anglican formularies, such as the Book of Common Prayer, the Thirty-Nine Articles of Religion and the Ordinal, together with the doctrinal parts of canon law, conspicuously avoid giving hostages to fanaticism, fundamentalism or dogmatism. The spirit of restraint inhibits these affirmations from becoming instruments of ideological oppression. But in their character as affirmation they are equally inhospitable to relativism, indifferentism and pragmatism. They do not convey the impression that the truth of the Christian faith and life is either unattainable or of secondary importance. These formularies reveal a Church or Communion quietly confident of its catholicity and apostolicity. If we can recover that godly confidence for ourselves, we shall indeed be keeping faith with Anglicanism.

Notes

1. *From Power to Partnership* (Church House Publishing, London, 1991), p.113.
2. W.M. Abbott, ed., *The Documents of Vatican II* (Geoffrey Chapman, London, 1966), p.23: *LG* 1.8.
3. ARCIC, *The Final Report* (SPCK/CTS, London, 1982), pp.86f; Abbott, ed., op. cit., p.364: *UR* III.22.
4. See further on this, P. Avis, *Christians in Communion* (Geoffrey Chapman-Mowbray/Liturgical Press, London, 1990), ch. 3.
5. *The Truth Shall Make you Free: The Lambeth Conference 1988* (Anglican Consultative Council, London, 1988), p.13.
6. C. Duquoc, *Provisional Churches* (SCM, London, 1986), p.90.
7. ibid., p.91.

8. *For the Conversion of the Churches* (WCC, Geneva, 1993).
9. Resolutions 48 and 49; see R. Coleman, *Resolutions of the Twelve Lambeth Conferences 1867-1988* (Anglican Book Centre, Toronto, 1992), pp.83ff.
10. S. Sykes and J. Booty, ed., *The Study of Anglicanism* (SPCK/Fortress, London, 1988), p.52.

The Problem of Authority

G.R. Evans

The phrase 'confessional identity' is sometimes used with a degree of pride by those who feel it right that it should be an ecclesial distinguishing mark for one set of Christians to hold beliefs which are somehow especially theirs. Such confessional identities have always arisen in the course in the course of separating from other Christians. They have become fixed in bodies of articles, such as the Church of England's Thirty-Nine Articles or the Lutheran Augsburg Confession of 1530, or the many collections of *loci communes*, or 'commonplaces', produced in the conflicts of the sixteenth century. There is another kind of 'special identity' to which a group of Christians may come to feel a special loyalty. This can be a 'style' of Churchmanship, and it is of course absolutely right that there should be richness and diversity here. But that is not inherently divisive and we need to be absolutely clear about the difference between making a claim to a distinctive orthodoxy in matters of faith and 'being ourselves' in the life of our own churches.

The English Anglican newspaper, the *Church Times* for April of this year,[1] contains the following advertisements, which could probably be matched, *mutatis mutandis*, in any week, in any part of the world. An organist is sought, who 'must be sympathetic to Catholic worship'. A youth worker is wanted, who is 'committed to Bible teaching and evangelism, to encourage and develop work with children and young people in this evangelical/renewal parish'. 'Central Churchmanship' crops up more than once, linked in one case with 'Vestments, Reserved Sacrament'. Elsewhere 'Conservative Evangelical Churchmen' are sought. The hard question is whether these advertisements are merely seeking to match a flavour of church life to the patterns of a given congregation, or pressing for something deeper and potentially divisive.

In the rather fearful climate in which Christians may seek to draw aside into a group of their own 'kind' within the Church, when things which are precious to them seem threatened, there can also be a focusing upon the negative, some matter or matters with which the group feels unhappy or which it disapproves of. Then it is important not to allow discontents to cluster, so that a number of other impressions and brooding disquiets about the way things are going become attached to one another. There can then be a danger of implying that 'if we let this or that happen there will be a landslide'. The tendency is for preferences and even prejudices to aggregate when a body of people find they share them; this is not the same thing as a true relationship of one to the other logically or theologically. There is a news item in the same number of the *Church Times* about the Anglican Evangelical Assembly, which describes the group as 'a conservative group initially formed around opposition to the ordination of women but far from shy about expressing opinions on other issues including gay clergy and quota capping'. There is here what might be called a 'grouping of views' which have in common simply their appeal to a certain kind of conservative temperament. Then we see the further pattern: 'Members ... have met in working groups over the last year to discuss what *they* [my italics] believe about the Church, ministry, mission, truth, worship and learning'. Groups similar to this have come into being lately, especially in those parts of the Anglican Communion where women's ordination has begun or been actively considered. Should those who find themselves forming one or moving into one stop and consider what they are doing? I think so. The common factor tends to be the sense that there is a threat to an old truth or practice. So other fears and threats join themselves together with that. Fear is a bad sign among Christians. Perfect love ought to cast it out (1 John 4.18).

The issue of 'authority' in the Anglican Communion has recently come to focus a good deal on the question whether we, or a proportion of us, geographically or otherwise defined, can make a decision independently of the rest, even if it will affect the rest in some material way. But we equally have to ask whether a group is entitled to try to set itself apart when that challenge arises. 'Geographically defined' means in practice 'provincially', for it is at provincial level that Anglicans make legislative decisions (The Church of England is a special case with its two provinces, but the rule about the local provincial character of legislation holds). 'Otherwise' might include party or group or even faction, what in the late Middle Ages would be called a *secta* – a group defining itself by a set of beliefs or practices it considers non-negotiable, and on which it is therefore not prepared to hold conversations with others.

It is a historical accident that Anglicans have provincial legislation. It arose in the different circumstances of the countries where Anglicanism was established. It became a 'conscious virtue' – if that is what it is – in Anglicanism only in the second half of the nineteenth century, with the forming of the first Lambeth Conference in 1867, and its motivation was much less ecclesiological than political. That is to say, the provinces were frightened of coming together in a framework where they could find themselves bound by a conciliar decision, and perhaps dominated by some of their number.

Taking a decision independently has always been acceptable in the Church's history where the principle of subsidiarity was properly applied, and especially where what was at issue was a difference of rite or practice not affecting Christians in other places and carrying no connotation of unorthodoxy of faith. The difference between autocephaly (the preferred Orthodox term) and autonomy (used by Anglicans in the phrase 'provincial autonomy') is important here. In Orthodoxy an autocephalous church is free from the jurisdiction of any other, and itself claims no jurisdiction over autocephalous sister-churches. It forms, sacramentally, a complete community which is fully the Church. But it does so on the understanding that it is a microcosm rather than a fragment of the whole. The structural difference is crucial. It also holds itself bound to maintain the common faith which is shared with the other autocephalous churches. Autonomy is different. It has to do with juridical or legislative rather than ecclesial independence. There is no defining sense of the sacramental completeness of each autonomous province. That has been our Anglican pattern. There is no underlying assumption of a bond of faith.

Much of the debate about authority has turned on whether a church or communion or ecclesial body, or a majority within it, has authority to do certain things when other bodies are not doing it and when the action cannot carry the whole community with it. Christians need now to give active thought to the question of authority to divide.

An Asian Christian has recently commented on

The power that resides in the churches of different traditions and confessions, and especially the power that both symbolically and in actuality is represented by church hierarchies. I may be wrong, but all along I had the suspicion that the question of power 'was kept at a respectful distance' (*chin er yuian chi*), to use a Chinese expression, in Church union negotiations, because it was a very sensitive question and might jeopardize an already precarious road to some form of church unity. But can a genuine unity of the churches be achieved without addressing it?[2]

I am afraid we have to be honest with ourselves about the fact that power-struggles are much in evidence in the attempts to resolve the present Anglican crises about authority.

Being official

What we are living through, and not only as Anglicans, is a crisis of 'reception'. Reception is the process by which the people of God comes to know its own mind under the guidance of the Holy Spirit, and because it is a human as well as a divine process it can feel very like muddle and look very like conflict, from the human viewpoint.

It is possible to bring about 'reception' of a sort by requiring the faithful to believe what they are told. Yet belief compelled must be in important ways different from belief freely given. This is a conflict at the heart of problems of authority in the Church. It can often be true, I fear, that when a group asks whether the Church has authority to do something, it means it wants to exercise authority to prevent it.

'Official' pronouncements seem on the face of it designed to require obedience. I use 'official' here to refer to decisions made and promulgated within the Church's formal structures, and carrying the sanction of the authority claimed for those structures.[3] Their authoritativeness is itself a vexed question, and what it consists in is one of the questions we have not begun to answer in the churches. But let us take it for now as 'given', and as a context for what is meant by their being 'official'.

There have always been teachers in the Church, and their teaching has normally been associated with leadership. Gregory the Great certainly saw the two roles as profoundly interconnected in the bishops who are the *rectores* of the Church. There are always also the taught, and those who are sheep to these shepherds. So there has been a tradition of obedience, compliance with teaching about the faith coming from above (*ob-audire* is 'to listen to', stresses the new Roman Catholic Catechism).[4] Leaders of the churches, usually acting together (for example, in synods and councils), have decreed canons of discipline and frameworks of order and (less often) made credal statements. (Of these the most important example is probably the Niceno-Constantinopolitan Creed framed by two Councils of the fourth century). These formulations have frequently been laid down with the intention of guiding, even directing the faithful.[5]

The good intentions of 'official' decision-making

The 'official' process has operated on the basis of high ideals of unanimity, consistency, continuity and faithfulness of witness to what has been held by all Christians always and everywhere. These ideals, with their greatness of vision and intention of rigour, have been consciously striven for and sustained in the formal processes.

The conciliar decision-making of the early Church consistently tried to ensure that what was being decided was in conformity with the faith of the gospel, with the decisions of previous councils and with the teachings of those who had been leaders and authorities in the community or who were the authors of texts the Church had come to respect. Cyril, Patriarch of Alexandria wrote to Nestorius at the Council of Ephesus of 431:

> The most effective way ... will be zealously to occupy ourselves with the words of the holy Fathers, to esteem their words, to examine our words *to see if we are holding to their faith*, as it is written (2 Cor.13.5), *to conform our thoughts* to their correct and irreproachable teaching.[6]

Similar sentiments were expressed at the Second Council of Constantinople in 553:

> We have driven off erroneous doctrines by *our collective resolution*, and we have renewed the unerring creed of the Fathers.[7]

The Council of Nicaea in 787 says in the same spirit:

> So it is that the teaching of our holy fathers is strengthened, namely, the tradition of the catholic Church which has received the gospel from one end of the earth to the other. So it is that we really follow Paul, who spoke in Christ, and the entire divine apostolic group and the holiness of the fathers, clinging fast to the traditions which we have received.[8]

In the primitive Councils such strongly expressed sentiments reflect an overriding concern for unity. Hence at Constantinople in 381 it is stated that,

> With the account of the faith agreed between us and with Christian love established among us, we shall cease to declare what was condemned by the apostles, 'I belong to Paul, I to Apollo, I to Cephas', but we shall be seen to belong to Christ, who has not been divided up among us; and with God's good favour, we shall keep the body of the church *undivided*, and shall come before the judgement-seat of the Lord with confidence.[9]

Here the original thrust of 'ecumenical' is clear and vigorous.

It is important to be conscious of the scale of the shift which took place with the divisions of the Church that arose from the East-West schism of 1054, and increasingly during and after the sixteenth century. These made it plain that a claim to faithfulness in continuity can also be made in separation. After the Reformation, we find claims of this sort in an Anglican context:

> The Church of Ireland doth, as heretofore, accept and unfeignedly believe all the Canonical[10] Scriptures[11] [and] doth continue to profess the faith of Christ as professed by the Primitive Church.[12]

It would be easy to multiply examples, especially of Western churches speaking since the sixteenth century, who would deem themselves to be sustaining this faithfulness in continuity with the primitive Church although they were divided from other contemporary churches to the point where they could not share the sacraments with them and perhaps even denied that they were churches at all.[13]

Yet in the early undivided Church not all councils were intended to be ecumenical in the sense of being universal. In fact, such councils were rare. Much more usual were meetings of bishops in a local region, designed to deal with a problem (often disciplinary), which had arisen locally and whose solution was of only local application. There was a well-established rule from an early date that a council had authority only over the local churches whose representatives had participated in it.[14] But it was accepted that there could be no legitimate local points of faith. In matters of faith only the universal would do. Any attempt to settle a dispute about the faith must therefore involve a universal or 'ecumenical' council, and be made with the intention that the decision should apply everywhere. It is in keeping with the rule of thinking on the largest possible scale of responsibility that independent creed-making was forbidden, as exemplified at the Council of Ephesus:

> It is not permitted to produce or write or compose any other creed except the one which was defined by the holy fathers who were gathered together in the Holy Spirit at Nicaea. Any who dare to compose or bring forth or produce another creed for the benefit of those who wish to turn from Hellenism or Judaism or some other heresy to the knowledge of the truth, if they are bishops or clerics they should be deprived of their respective charges and if they are laymen they are to be anathematized.[15]

But the circumstances in which a decision has been made formally and officially with the intention of settling a disputed point of faith once and for all have arisen relatively infrequently. Less than two dozen councils have called themselves 'ecumenical';[16] or been summoned at the instigation of the Western patriarchate as 'Lateran' or 'Vatican'[17] Councils with the intention of being ecumenical (as far as was possible in circumstances of schism); or else have been held (as Lyons 1274 and Ferrara-Florence in the early fifteenth century) with the purpose of making it possible for the schism of 1054 between East and West to be mended. Not all these councils have dealt with disputed points of faith. For example, the first three Lateran Councils were almost entirely concerned with other matters, and the Fourth Lateran Council devoted only a small (though crucially important) proportion of its texts to the subject.

By contrast, in the divided churches of the post-Reformation period we find talk of decisions made 'officially' by 'this Church'[18] or that, on points touching the faith. The Evangelical-Lutheran Church of Finland, for example, can say that it 'holds as the highest law of the confession' and mean by that the highest law of the faith as set out in its own Confession.[19] It is possible for another church to speak of 'The faith, confession and doctrine of the Church of Sweden.'[20] This is not to imply that these are necessarily thought to be matters of faith exclusive to the churches in question. It is rather that they are seen as 'the true faith' held secure in a given community. These too reflect, then, a universal intent and a concern to demonstrate unanimity with the primitive faith but coupled with a mistrust of the faithfulness of some or all other communities.

When a disputed point of faith has been discussed by a conciliar body there has almost always been a foregoing debate which has made it seem necessary, the asking of questions on a significant point of faith, often by a persistent individual who seems likely to mislead the faithful and indeed begins to form a group around himself. Arius is an obvious case in point.[21] Declarations made in the divided churches too, have often been prompted by an existing debate, but the perception of the nature of the prompter is different. A whole ecclesial community is deemed to have gone astray in its belief and practice in some way, or even all others except the one making the declaration, so that it becomes necessary for a remnant[22] to preserve the integrity of the faith.

The intention of permanence and faithfulness in continuity, goes with the intention of universality. 'The profession of faith of the holy fathers who gathered in Nicaea in Bithynia [325] is not to be abrogated, but it is to remain in force.'[23] It is a principle to be found everywhere in 'official' decision-making on points of faith that the decision is intended to stand indefinitely; this is as true of decisions in the divided churches as of earlier 'ecumenical' decision-making. It is also intended from at least the Council of Nicaea of 325, that a credal formulation shall be complete. The Third Council of Constantinople in 680-1 reflects that the Nicene Creed ought to have 'been enough for a complete knowledge of the orthodox faith and a complete assurance therein', and so settle things, but Satan does not rest and new problems arise.[24] Completeness remained an ideal; repetition and revision the reality.[25]

It was not in question in the early Church that there should be unanimity. The Letter of the Synod of Constantinople (381) to the Emperor Theodosius describes how 'first of all' the bishops had 'renewed unity of heart each with the other'. The same Council's Synodical Letter to the Bishops assembled at Rome declares that its 'disposition is all for peace with unity as its sole object' and that it writes 'with common consent'. The Synodal Letter of the Council of Antioch in 431 had spoken of 'joining together in unity of mind and concord and the spirit of peace'. At Chalcedon in 451 it is intended 'that all ambiguity be taken away, by the agreement and consent of all the holy fathers, and by their united exposition and doctrine'. When he composed his letter on the Paschal controversy, Cummianus, abbot of Iona (d.?669) was able to assemble a great many patristic authorities in support of unanimity. The episcopal role was essentially collective, though it was also true that individual bishops carried a special authority in their writings. A high proportion of the ancient Fathers of the Church were bishops.

It was understood from an early date that this unanimity of those with responsibility for guardianship of the faith keeps the faith unblemished. It is the means of 'cutting off every heresy', as the Synodal Letter of Nicaea in 325 puts it. At Ephesus in 431 the Synod received a letter from Pope Celestine stressing the bishops' duty to keep uncorrupt 'in common the faith which has come down to us today, through the apostolic succession'; 'let us be unanimous, thinking the same thing, for this is expedient ... let us be in all things of one mind, of one heart, when the faith, which is one, is attacked'.[26] This twofold conception of the function of unanimity thus created a habit of thinking in terms of acceptance and rejection, and with it the fundamentally adversarial pattern which has been persistent and destructive in the history of reception-processes. The motif becomes one of obedience or refusal of obedience to what is laid down.

Structural features of official decision-making

We must move now from the good intentions to the devising of structures. This is most markedly where elements of compulsion can enter into the process with the accompanying sanctions. That which is formally enacted by due process in a properly constituted authoritative body with the stamp of authority is normally deemed to have lawfulness. (Though legislative force may need to be ratified by the secular government in some times and places.)[27] This is often seen as tied both to proper constitutional procedure and to a known date and place of enactment. For example, in the Church of Ireland it is stated, 'And this Church will continue to use the same, subject to such alterations only as may be made therein from time to time *by the lawful authority* of the Church'.[28] The Church of Norway has as its confessional basis *by a law* of 1687 the Apostles' Creed, the Niceno-Constaninopolitan Creed, the Athanasian Creed and the Augsburg Confession of 1530. Luther's Small Catechism[29] is 'explicated and elucidated in The Book of Concord and other documents *approved by* the Church of Sweden'.[30] This 'lawfulness' will make the enactment binding to a degree dependent on the way it is 'set up' to be binding. Of these by far the most usual in the history of the Church has been exclusion from the community, either by excommunication, so that the breaker of the law is shut out from the sacraments, or by some other form of banning, such as refusal to speak to or eat with him or her. In the Roman Catholic *Veritatis Splendor* of 1993 we find simply but imperatively: 'The Church's magisterium ... teaches the faithful specific particular precepts and *requires* that they consider them in conscience as morally binding.'[31]

It is not, however, always clear in texts stressing authoritativeness in this way where 'lawfulness' of this sort ends and divine sanction begins:

> This synod, *legitimately* assembled *in the Holy Spirit*, constituting a general council, representing the catholic church militant, has *power immediately from Christ*, and that everyone of whatever state or dignity, even papal, is bound to *obey* it in those matters which pertain to the faith and the eradication of the said schism.[32]

The urge to claim that proper procedures and due process have been followed seems to reflect the need to be able to point incontrovertibly to 'where' and 'when'; the sanction of the Holy Spirit and the gift of Christ's authority arguably cannot, by their very nature, be used in this way because they are gifts of grace and therefore actively at God's disposal.[33]

There is a tension here between the finished, and the open-ended; the human and limited, and the divine with its infinite possibilities of surprise. This is an aspect of the paradox of 'official' decision-making, that the 'official' cannot easily be matched with the tidal ebb and flow of the wholeness of the reception-process as it involves everyone.

What, then, with these provisos, have been the patterns of decision-making structures? The letter of the Synod of Nicaea 325 to the Egyptians stresses that the Council has been called together from different provinces and cities to 'constitute' the great and holy synod.[34] A principle which scarcely needs to be underlined here is that decisions about the faith ought properly to be made by the whole Church ('whole' in quantity or extendedness) in the Holy Spirit (who assures its sanctity), and that means that representatives of as much of it as possible have to be brought together to form the council, so as to make the meeting as comprehensive a test-bed of the Spirit's intention as possible. (Doubts about the outcome of the deliberations of the first Vatican Council increased when the number of absentee bishops became known.)[35]

So official decision-making has classically involved a conciliar process, defined as one in which the leaders of the local churches in particular[36] have met to take counsel together and agree on a decision. Their positions of local leadership, and especially their episcopal relationship to their communities as ministers of oversight, are seen as giving weight to their deliberations. For many centuries, throughout most of the Christian world, the persons who have a special responsibility in the Church for teaching and the maintenance of the faith were taken to be bishops (*episcopoi*), especially when they made a pronouncement together in this way in a synod or council. That has continued in the divided churches where an episcopal structure has been maintained. Thus, 'received and approved by the archbishops and bishops and the rest of the clergy of Ireland in the synod holden in Dublin, A.D. 1634,'[37] is a way of giving official status to a declaration of the Church of Ireland. The principle holds strongly in modern Roman Catholic documents.

Once they had evolved, the assumptions we are exploring as to what constituted 'official' decision-making remained relatively constant for the first fifteen hundred years of the Church's life. Bishops met, representing their local churches.[38] Thus the whole Church could be held to meet in unity. If a smaller geographical area than the whole Church was represented, the decisions of the resulting council applied only to the area in question. No part of the Church could bind another without the other being present and consenting.[39]

But with the Reformation of the sixteenth century and its consequent divisions, something new began to happen. The structure of local churches with leaders who are all bishops, and bishops in the same way, with the same understanding of the nature and role of the episcopate, broke down. New polities were set up, some led by ministers who refused to consider themselves in any sense episcopal. The old patterns of succession in the ministry were disrupted.[40]

Leaders of local churches in the alternative polities devised from the sixteenth century did not stand in the same relationship of focus and representation as bishops to their people. Changes of structure (and, perhaps more importantly, of ideology about that structure) in many of the reforming communities, were calling into question the viability of such conciliar patterns. It became much more difficult to say what 'conciliarity' meant in the polities of churches which did not have bishops. The conciliar pattern, in which bishops act as guardians of the faith and spokesmen for their communities, depended on the continuance of the traditional episcopate. This disappeared in the Radical Reformation, in the Reformed tradition, and partly in Lutheranism and Methodism, in favour of conceptions of all-member ministry, of gathered churches appointing their own local ministers to hold an office (not an order)[41] for a limited period. That destroyed or altered various understandings of the way in which, when bishops met in council, the whole Church could be said to be meeting in its representatives.[42]

At first in the sixteenth-century crisis a Council was called for, as a means of common and official decision-making about the need for reform. It was long and painfully delayed, and by the time the Council of Trent met it was no longer possible for the whole community to come together, but only for the reformers and dissidents to be, as it were, summoned before the Council to give account of themselves. It has never since been possible to hold a Council which would, even in principle, be a Council of the whole Church.

Within some of those churches which retained an episcopal structure and which could still hold Councils in the traditional way (except that they could no longer be deemed ecumenical), a fresh series of developments has been at work, especially in the last century or so. These have, again, begun to alter the understanding on which the whole Church can be deemed to make a decision in and with its bishops, and therefore by a process within which the leadership instructs the faithful in the faith, and can require their obedience to what they are taught.

The most notable changes within the episcopal system have been in the role of the laity in the 'official process'. A House of Clergy had sat with the House of Bishops in the Church of England since the Middle Ages. It was always the junior House and dependent upon the House of Bishops to allow it to make its contribution to the decision-making process. From the nineteenth century there were calls to allow the laity to have a part in the process of consultation. In the early nineteenth century John Henry Newman wrote to his friend Hurrell Froude, 'I want your view of the extent of power which may be given to the laity in the Church system, e.g. the maintenance of the Faith is their clear prerogative. Question. What power may they have in synods? Judicially? In legislation? etc'.[43] There were already questions about procedure and enfranchisement here which are only gradually being resolved even in the twentieth century.

In England Henry Hoare and the Society for the Revival of Convocation did not think the laity ought to be included in the synodical process but took a lead in encouraging their participation at parish level and in rural deaneries. The result was a growing pattern of co-operation between clergy and laity in the running of the church. In 1884 there was a proposal to set up 'Houses' of laymen,[44] to meet simultaneously with clerical Houses in their Convocation and to be consulted about 'the definition or interpretation of the faith and doctrine of the Church'.[45] The first session of the Canterbury House of Laymen was opened in January 1886, that of York not until 1892. There were proposals for a national Synod of Laymen, with the result that in 1898 the two provincial Houses of Laymen met together in London.

In conception these 'Houses' of laymen were advisory. They were therefore not attractive to the lay membership because they had no authority and could not participate in legislation.[46] Attendance was poor. The Report of the 1898 Joint Committee to consider the position of the laity recommended the setting up of a National Council to represent the clergy and laity. A Representative Church Council emerged from this in 1903, but it was still deliberative, and without legislative functions. A new Commission was set up in 1913, under the presidency of Lord Selborne. This proposed, when it reported in 1916, that a Church Council should be brought into being, consisting of the two Houses of the Convocations and a House of Laity.[47] This was the origin of the Church Assembly, the ancestor of the present General Synod.[48] But that involved a shift of principle. The bishops of the early local churches meeting in council are deemed to 'bring their churches with them'.[49] The new 'representatives by election' could not do so in the same way, and indeed the two modes of 'representation' must inevitably coexist somewhat uneasily. There is the further danger that the use of the same word for two different relationships of 'representation' can be confusing and 'send out the wrong signals'.

So in a House system the local churches are no longer the natural focus, as the primary ecclesial entities entering into discussion with one another, and trying to reach decisions together. The old rules of unanimity and universal intent can easily be lost sight of in a system of majority voting. Interest groups and 'parties' can arise which put 'universal intention' out of focus. Decisions can be made for short-term reasons or out of 'party interest', and so the intentions of permanence and completeness are weakened. The continuance of a 'conciliar' system of official decision-making, even in a church which has preserved an episcopal polity, can thus become uncertain in its continuity of purpose. And, more importantly, with lay participation in such decision-making on the basis of a different kind of representation, the boundary between 'official' decision-making by leaders in the Church and a process of reception in which all the faithful actively share, becomes blurred.

Consultation in official decision-making

The conciliar process has not always involved actual problem-solving. Nevertheless, 'official' decisions were in principle and intention arrived at by the pooling of opinions, the real forming of a common mind. At the Second Council of Constantinople (553),

> They dealt with heresies and current problems by debate in common, since it was established as certain that when the disputed question is set out by each side in communal discussions, the light of truth drives out the shadows of lying. The truth cannot be made clear in any other way when there are debates about questions of faith, since *everyone* requires the assistance of his neighbour.[50]

At the Council of Constance, session 1, November, 1414, the Pope called for the active assistance of everyone:

> Considering, moreover, that a council should specially treat of those matters which concern the catholic faith, according to the praise-worthy practices of the early councils, and aware that such things demand diligence, sufficient time and study, on account of their difficulty, we therefore exhort all those who are well versed in the sacred scriptures to ponder and to treat, both within themselves and with others, about those things which seem to them useful... Let them bring such things to our notice and to that of this sacred synod, as soon as they conveniently can, so that at a suitable time there may be decided what things, it seems, should be held and what repudiated for the profit and increase of the same catholic faith... We exhort, moreover, all catholics assembled here and others who will come to this sacred synod that they should seek to think on, to follow up and to bring to us, and to this same sacred

synod, those matters by which the body of catholics may be led, if God is willing, to a proper reformation and to the desired peace. For it is our intention and will that all who are assembled for this purpose may say, consult about and do, with complete freedom, each and all of the things that they think pertain to the above.[51]

Consultation could be unwieldy, however. The Constitutions of the Second Council of Lyons, 1274, express gratitude that so many

Patriarchs, primates, archbishops, bishops, abbots, priors, provosts, deans, archdeacons and other prelates of churches, both personally and by suitable procurators, and the procurators of chapters, colleges and convents, have assembled at our call.

But they ask for understanding that 'although for the happy pursuit of so great an enterprise their advice would be useful, and their presence as beloved sons is so delightful', that presence presents problems. They are a jostling crowd. However, 'their absence may be harmful to themselves and their churches'. So it is decided that those who have been specifically invited shall stay on, 'patriarchs, primates, archbishops, bishops, abbots and priors'.[52] Some of the calls for active consultation were undoubtedly window-dressing, or had a political purpose. But the intention is clear, that there should be sharing of thoughts and an attempt to win one another's minds in unanimity.

Similarly, the sharing of thoughts is extended to the announcement of the Council's decisions. From Nicaea 325, the letter of the Synod to the Egyptians further explains that the council needs to send a letter 'so that you may know what was proposed and discussed and what was decided and enacted (*quae vera placita*)'. There is concern to make the local application plain. 'These are the chief and most important decrees as far as concerns Egypt ... Alexander will tell you more when he comes' for he was himself a leader as well as a participant in the events.[53] This rule of openness has remained important, and when there has been suspicion that it has been broken, that has sometimes been thought to invalidate the synodical process.

Frequency or regularity of meeting was not a noticeable characteristic of early councils. On the contrary, they tended to be extraordinary events. The Council of Basle (December, 1431), claims the warrant of Constance (1415) for 'the frequent holding of general councils'.[54] But that was principally because its own meeting came so soon after, and is a testimony to its extraordinary nature rather than to the claim about the frequency of general councils. The modern call for more frequent meetings reflects a desire for democracy to be seen to operate. This is a kind of ecclesiastical equivalent of 'no taxation without representation'.

The modern scene

A unanimous vote was achieved at the Faith and Order Conference held in Edinburgh in 1937 by 414 delegates. The size and geographical spread of this number was emphasised in much the way it might have been in one of the early ecumenical councils:

> The Second World Conference on Faith and Order, held at Edinburgh in August 1937, brought together four hundred and fourteen delegates from one hundred and twenty-two Christian communions in forty-three different countries. The delegates assembled to discuss together the causes that keep Christian communions apart, and the things that unite them in Christian fellowship. The Conference approved the following statement *nemine contradicente*.[55]

But the Edinburgh Conference, although it found itself of one mind on certain points, was not a council, and did not aspire to be. That is to say, it did not purport to be a meeting of all the churches in their representatives with the intention of arriving at conclusions binding on them all. It could not make decisions which it could oblige participants to obey.

A very recent Roman Catholic document is confident that such a meeting can, despite these limitations, do other things of value in advancing the reception-process, such as bear 'witness' and 'give the stamp of authenticity':

> Meetings of authorised representatives of Churches and ecclesial Communities can help greatly to promote ecumenical co-operation. As well as being an important witness to the commitment of those who participate in the promotion of Christian unity, they can give the stamp of authenticity to the co-operative efforts of members of the Churches and ecclesial Communities they represent. They may also provide the occasion for examining what specific questions and tasks of ecumenical co-operation need to be addressed and for taking necessary decisions about the setting up of working groups or programmes to deal with them.[56]

Nevertheless, there is still a substantial difference between the aspirations of an early ecumenical council to speak for the whole Church, and what such a modern meeting of the divided churches can do.

Early 'official' decisions were often made with the intention that they should be accepted as a matter of obedience by the faithful who were not present and directly involved. The Council of Ephesus of 431 in its synodical letter to the eastern bishops says that even if any bishop was not able to be at the synod he should still know what it decided and obey.[57]

There is, therefore, a difficulty. If the intention of official declarations is that they should at a given point determine on behalf of the community what the community must then accept, that would appear to be incompatible with a participatory and gradual process. Now these are not incompatible processes if the 'official' decision always gets it right. It can then be argued that the free process of arriving at consensus will, under the guidance of the Holy Spirit, in the end come up with the same view of the one faith as the official machinery, if that is also under the guidance of the Holy Spirit. But if there is any possibility of even short-term error, or incompleteness in the working of the 'official' system, we must postulate that the forming of a participatory consensus is not merely a correlative to the framing of official decisions, but sometimes a shaper of it, sometimes a corrective to it, sometimes a completion of it: 'Revelation is already complete' yet 'it has not been made completely explicit; it remains for Christian faith gradually to grasp its full significance over the course of the centuries'.[58]

The current Anglican situation

There are uncomfortable things to think about in our own motivation when we find ourselves placing stumbling-blocks in one another's way. It is important to try to be honest about how far the tensions of a given situation, internally within a single church or ecumenically between churches, have to do with fear of loss of status, fear of loss of effective authority, fear that all we hold dear is being traded away and with it our own position, or fear of loss of control. These are familiar patterns in microcosm of the breakdown of personal relationships. We have to be able to learn to recognise them in the breakdown of ecclesial relationships, too.

The Eames Commission, faced with the *de facto* loss of mutual recognition of ministries which followed upon the ordination of women in some provinces of the Anglican Communion and not others, saw it as its brief 'to discover the language and context in which Anglicans can continue to live together'.[59] 'The loss of the universal acceptance of ordained ministers and of their interchangeability across provincial boundaries is seen as a difficulty that will seriously affect the texture of inter-provincial relationships',[60] is a statement of fact not of policy. That is simply how it is.

There is discussion in the *First Report* of the Eames Commission of the rules by which partial communion has worked out in practice.[61] It also explored the idea of communion as having degrees,[62] and as broken or impaired, and appealed to the fact that 'there has never been a time when ecclesial communion has perfectly reflected the unity which is both God's gift and promise'.[63] That was perhaps necessary in the interests of damage limitation, but it seems to me an unhelpful line to pursue if it can lead to *acceptance* of something less than the real thing in the long term. There is a world of difference between seeing ourselves as moving from the broken, partial and incomplete to the perfection of communion, and accepting that we can go backwards towards a lower degree of communion than we had before and settle for that. Such a situation must be regarded as an emergency, an interim. The historically familiar device of the emergency measure is used by the Eames Commission. So, for example, in defending its suggestions about the provision of Episcopal Visitors it states that 'From an ecclesiological perspective such a scheme can be defended, as a necessary and strictly extraordinary anomaly in preference to schism, if certain conditions are met'.[64] I would like to argue that the ecclesial thrust in an ecumenical age must always be centripetal not centrifugal.

The Commission tried to build on what remained in common during this emergency. It spoke of: 'Mutual recognition of the partners as belonging together in the one Body of Christ through faith and baptism.' 'From this' it is suggested 'that what the partners have in common is more important than what divides. Precisely because the other partner also belongs to Christ, they must be accorded an integrity which commands respect and courtesy. This will include a recognition of the ecclesial integrity of the intention of the partner'.[65] Most importantly, there is a warning in Eames that, although at the level of the interchangeability of ministries there is now a lesser degree of communion, this 'must not tempt Anglicans into thinking that communion is only to be defined in terms of the interchangeability of ministries.'[66]

The term 'partner' needs scrutiny here. 'Respect',[67] and 'courtesy'[68] are cool words in comparison with 'love', but they are on the right side. They express a cautious possibility of movement together – cautious because of the sheer uncertainty about how to go forward and where to go next in this situation. 'In the continuing and dynamic process of reception, freedom and space must be available until a consensus of opinion one way or the other has been achieved'.[69] What is being maintained is that within an open process of reception there is inevitably a provisionality about the development itself.[70] Mere federation[71] is seen to be unsatisfactory.

There is a real sense within this struggle of the huge demands communion makes, and a clear willingness to settle ultimately for nothing less than the real thing in the recognition that all 'should consider carefully what anomalies they are prepared to accept for the sake of unity'.[72] I myself would have to say that unity is of supreme importance. That is what we have to hang on to, and one doubts whether we can ever have authority to do anything else.

Notes

1. 28 April 1995.
2. Choan-Seng Song, *Encounters for Unity* (Norwich, 1995), p.37.
3. Historically these have been most usually councils or synods.
4. *Catechism of the Catholic Church*, 144 (Rome, 1994), p.36.
5. The Second Vatican Council still says 'The task of authentically interpreting the word of God, whether in its written form or in that of tradition, has been entrusted only to those charged with the church's ongoing teaching function (*solo vivo ecclesiae magisterio concreditum est*), whose authority is exercised in the name of Jesus Christ. Vatican II, *De divina revelatione*, II.10, *Decrees of the Ecumenical Councils*, Norman P. Tanner (Georgetown, 1990), II.975.
6. Council of Ephesus, 431, Second letter of Cyril to Nestorius, Tanner, I.40–1. (author's italics).
7. Second Council of Constantinople, 553, 'Sentence against the Three Chapters', Tanner I.108 (author's italics).
8. Second Council of Nicaea, 787, 'Definition', Tanner, I.136.
9. Council of Constantinople, 381, Tanner, I.30 (author's italics).
10. This is a reference to the sixteenth-century debate on the inclusion of the Apocrypha.
11. The Constitution of the Church of Ireland, adopted by the General Convention in the year 1870: Preamble and Declaration, *Together in Mission and Ministry: the Porvoo Common Statement with Essays in Church and Ministry in Northern Europe, Conversations between the British and Irish Anglican Churches and the Nordic and Baltic Lutheran Churches* (London, 1993), pp.186-7.
12. ibid.
13. See my *The Church and the churches* (Cambridge, 1994), Chapter 1.
14. That is one reason for the concern of those councils which did want to be thought of as ecumenical to make efforts to declare their universal authority when it had not in fact been the case that every bishop had been present.
15. Council of Ephesus, 431, Tanner, I.65.
16. Constantinople, 868-70 is an example of a council not recognised by the East, Tanner, I.137.
17. This is in contrast to summoning by Emperors in early centuries, and by 'princes' and 'magistrates' in the sixteenth-century Reformation.
18. The Constitution of the Church of Ireland, adopted by the General

Convention in the year 1870: Preamble and Declaration, *Together in Mission and Ministry: the Porvoo Common Statement with Essays in Church and Ministry in Northern Europe, Conversations between the British and Irish Anglican Churches and the Nordic and Baltic Lutheran Churches*, pp.186-7.

19. ibid., pp.189-90.
20. ibid., p.189.
21. See R. Williams' recent study, *Arius* (London, 1987).
22. See *The Church and the churches*, Chapter 2.
23. Tanner, I.31.
24. Third Council of Constantinople, 680-1, Tanner, I.125.
25 In the 'modern doctrinal writings which are held to be of authority in the eastern Church', *Answers of the Patriarch Jeremiah to the Lutherans*, should be compared with Acts and XVIII Articles of the Synod of Bethlehem in relation to Calvinist teaching. The Eastern Churches had had no need to promulgate any new creeds from the time of John Damascene. See *The Doctrine of the Russian Church*, tr. R.W. Blackmore (Aberdeen, 1845), p.xv.
26. Labbe, *Concilia*, III.613.
27. The Church of England is an example.
28. The Constitution of the Church of Ireland, adopted by the General Convention in the year 1870: Preamble and Declaration, *Together in Mission and Ministry: the Porvoo Common Statement with Essays in Church and Ministry in Northern Europe, Conversations between the British and Irish Anglican Churches and the Nordic and Baltic Lutheran Churches*, pp.186-7 (author's italics).
29. ibid., p.189.
30. ibid., p.192 (author's italics).
31. See *Veritatis Splendor*: 'In addition, the Magisterium carries out an important work, of vigilance, warning the faithful of possible errors, even merely implicit ones, when their *consciences* fail to acknowledge the correctness and the truth of the moral norms which the Magisterium teaches... Moral theologians are to set forth the Church's teaching and to give, in the exercise of their ministry, the example of a loyal assent, both external and internal, to the Magisterium's teaching in the areas of both dogma and morality', 110 (author's italics).
32. Council of Constance, March, 1415, Abbreviation read aloud by Cardinal Zabarella, Tanner I.408 (author's italics).
33. That God cannot be bound by rules of human devising is a principle famously stressed by Gregory the Great in the sixth century.
34. Tanner, I.17-18.
35. F.M. Bliss, *Understanding Reception: a background to its ecumenical use* (Rome, 1991), p.108.
36. And latterly representatives who are themselves lay-people.
37. The Constitution of the Church of Ireland, adopted by the General Convention in the year 1870: Preamble and Declaration, *Together in Mission and Ministry: the Porvoo Common Statement with Essays in*

Church and Ministry in Northern Europe, Conversations between the British and Irish Anglican Churches and the Nordic and Baltic Lutheran Churches, pp.186-7.

38. Under the leadership of one of their number who was senior by virtue of the 'metropolitan' character of the see he held. The calling of councils by emperors, princes and magistrates has a long history which there is not space to go into here. Such leadership has never by tradition interfered with doctrinal decision-making.

39. We have already noted that this was acted on in spirit rather than to the letter in the case of the great ecumenical councils of the early Church, where a rather unbalanced spread of bishops was actually present in each case, but where it was clearly intended that they should decide on behalf of the whole Church.

40. See *The Church and the churches*, Chapter 4.

41. On the difference, see *Episcopal Ministry, Report of the Archbishop's Group on the Episcopate* (London, 1990), pp.59ff.

42. But see my *Problems of Authority in the Reformation Debates* (Cambridge, 1992), p.246.

43. *Letters and Correspondence of John Henry Newman during his life in the English Church*, ed., Anne Mozley (London, 1891), Vol.II.110.

44. Not of course yet of women.

45. *Chronicle of Convocation* (1877, 1884, 1885, with resolutions agreed July, 1885 (xxx.244-65; xxxi.270-4).

46. Even those within the 'official' process can feel they have no effect if they are not allowed to legislate. That is what happened when the Convocations were revived in England in the middle of the nineteenth century, but were not at first given the royal licence for revision of a canon. On 26 February 1861, Dr Tait said in the Upper House of Convocation, 'although we knew that it was very desirable that we should have the opportunity of meeting and expressing our opinions, and although we knew also that the opinions so expressed might often be of great influence on the country in general, yet still we did not feel that we were allowed to proceed with any real matter of business.' *Chronicle of Convocation* (1861), p.346.

47. *The Archbishops' Committee on Church and State, Report* (London, 1916).

48. *Episcopal Ministry*, pp.101.ff.

49. This was the theme of the Lambeth Conference of 1988.

50. Second Council of Constantinople, 553, 'Sentence against the Three Chapters', Tanner I.108 (author's italics).

51. Tanner, I.406.

52. Tanner, I.313.

53. Tanner, I.17-18.

54. Constance, Tanner I.438-9, Basle, Tanner I.455.

55. *Creeds of the Churches*, ed., John H. Leith (Virginia, 1963 revised edn., 1973), p.572-3, 'With no one dissenting' seems to have a different force from that of 'everyone agreeing'.

56. Vatican, *Ecumenical Directory*, para.164.
57. Council of Ephesus, 431, Tanner, I.163.
58. *Catechism of the Catholic Church* (London, 1994), para.66, p.22.
59. *The Eames Commission: the Official Reports*, Anglican Consultative Council (Toronto, 1994), First Report, 1989, 5, p.12.
60. *The Eames Commission, Fourth meeting*, 1990, 53, p.65.
61. *The Eames Commission, First Report*, 1989, 33, p.19.
62. *The Eames Commission, Second Report*, 1989, 7, p.45.
63. *The Eames Commission, First Report*, 1989, 31, p.18.
64. *The Eames Commission, First Report*, 1989, 55, p.30.
65. *The Eames Commission, First Report*, 1989, 33, p.19.
66. *The Eames Commission, First Report*, 1989, 59, p.32.
67. *The Eames Commission, Second Report*, 1989, 3, p.43, 6, p.44.
68. *The Eames Commission, Second Report*, 1989, 3, p.43.
69. *The Eames Commission, First Report*, 1989, 43, p.24.
70. *The Eames Commission, Clarifications*, p.54.
71. *The Eames Commission, First Report*, 59, p.32.
72. *The Eames Commission, First Report*, 64, p.33.

Order and the Episcopate

John Halliburton

At St Paul's Cathedral, there is a tradition that each November, the Moderator of the Church of Scotland is invited to lunch with the Dean and Chapter. The Moderator is rather more splendidly attired than the average Anglican bishop with even a modest purple glowing from beneath his lace ruff and frock coat. He remains nonetheless wedded to the presbyterian order and on one occasion, the Moderator of the year, realising that my name is Scottish, asked me about my father. Was he an Episcopalian clergyman? No, I said, he was a good Church of Scotland banker, lived in the south, married a Church of England wife and brought me up as an Anglican. The Moderator thought for a moment. 'Ay', he said, 'there is such a thing as a fall from grace'. Sometimes I think he was right. Looking at the episcopate, not only within Anglicanism but wherever it exists, looking at the tangles over Church unity which are so heavily embarrassed by the tangles over ministerial order, I do from time to time look wistfully at the lovely and dramatic Scottish scenery and wish I were back in somewhere like Crieff where my grandfather lived and where the only purple around was in the heather. A church without bishops, what bliss!

A church where the presbyters meet in grave and learned council, where each has parity with the other, and where there are no higher or lower orders of ministry – is not this really the New Testament pattern where presbyter equals bishop and bishop equals presbyter? Was it not presbyters, possibly in the plural, that the apostles appointed in every place?[1] Was it not the presbyters who laid hands on Timothy ('Neglect not the gift that is in you by the laying on of hands of the presbytery')[2] in order to appoint him to the care of the local church? Did not the presbyters of Alexandria really get it right when, as tradition has it, at the instigation of St Mark a college of twelve of them regularly consecrated their own bishop until about the year 250?[3] Was it not this precedent that encouraged, more than a

39

thousand years later, the divines of the German Reformation to abandon the resident episcopate and appoint their own pastors, who in turn would corporately as a body elect and ordain their own superintendent minister, later to be known as a bishop?   Anyone studying the sixteenth-century church orders of Brandenburg and Lower Saxony cannot fail to be left with the impression that the churches reformed by Luther and his associates founded their restructuring of ministerial order on the conviction that it was the presbyterate that out of necessity created the order of the episcopate or superintendent (in the letters of Dr Bugenhagen of Wittenberg, prominent in the history of the Reformation in Denmark, these terms were interchangeable)[4]; and that it was the presbyterate that both elected and appointed their own superior.

When Bugenhagen himself was elected superintendent minister for Brunswick, being then chief pastor of Wittenberg, he insisted that his appointment should be in the traditional manner. Accordingly, the church in Wittenberg arranged for the pastors of the chief churches in Wittenberg to lay hands on him with prayer.[5] It was a repeat of what they thought happened in Alexandria in the fourth century. It affirmed their belief in the episcopate; but it also underlined their conviction that the episcopate was a development of the presbyterate, as the archbishop is the product of the provincial council of bishops. In the beginning, there was only one ordained ministry of oversight and that was the presbyter, sometimes called a bishop. The bishop, i.e. the superintendent minister, governing a group of churches, emerged subsequently to meet pastoral need. Despite the dignity of his position and responsibility, he is answerable to his own electorate and to the people of God who chose him and, through their pastoral ministers, appointed him.

In a world in which some had grown tired of the pyramid of royalty and feudalism, this must have been a very tempting exegesis. Sadly, it does not fully accommodate the evidence. The account is seriously flawed by the clear fact that it is the apostles who appointed the presbyter/bishops of the New Testament era[6] and that it was these who not only appointed successors for each local church[7] but who in fact created the order of presbyters as we now know it. In Luke's account in Acts 14.23, it is clearly the apostles Paul and Barnabas who appoint presbyters in every church and (in Acts 20.28) assign to them the ministry of oversight (*episkopē*). In the pastoral epistles, it is again evident that it is the author who calls himself the apostle Paul who lays hands on Timothy to appoint him to office and that Timothy also lays hands on others (II Tim. 1.6; I Tim. 5.22); the reference to the 'laying on of hands with the presbytery' in I Tim. 4.14 is taken by some to refer to the rugby scrum of clergy suffocating the candidate for ordination to either the episcopate or the presbyterate in the modern church, and was strongly appealed to by those contending that the bishop was ordained by presbyters. We cannot however detach this text from the author, Paul's assertion that he, an apostle, bestowed the gift on Timothy by the laying on of 'my hands'. David Daube, writing in *The New Testament and Rabbinic Judaism*[8] rightly points out that the laying on of hands is not 'of the presbyters' (plural i.e. a crowd of presbyters) but 'of the presbytery'; and he goes on further to say that the phrase 'when the council of elders laid their hands on you' is a technical expression for the act of ordination, and has nothing to do with presbyters actually laying on hands. The ordination of Timothy to the care of the local church was by the apostle Paul; the elders (they may even have been presbyter/bishops) as a council may or may not have taken part. But they were certainly not solely responsible for Timothy's appointment. Further, Clement of Rome (who is often discounted because he is not in the New Testament canon but is in fact somewhat earlier than the last books of the New Testament) records the tradition of the church of his time that the apostles,

> as they preached in the country and in the towns, they appointed their first-fruits ... to be bishops and deacons of them that should believe ... our Apostles knew also through our Lord Jesus Christ, that there would be strife over the dignity of the bishop's office. For this reason, therefore, having received complete foreknowledge, they appointed the aforesaid, and after a time made provision that on their death, other approved men should succeed to their ministry.[9]

The episcopate, in other words, is the original order; and it is from this order that the order which came to be called the presbyterate devolves.

At the turn of the first century, therefore, we have a picture developing (as, for example in the Letters of Ignatius of Antioch)[10] of one bishop serving a local Christian community which by that time was probably so scattered around the city in various house churches that the bishop needed to send delegates to cope with Sunday worship, pastoral care and instruction. For this purpose, he ordained presbyters who went out as needed at the bishop's bidding. They were his council and his counsellors,[11] trusted men of good report. But probably most important in the bishop's *familia* was the deacon. We hear a lot said about deacons being willing servants who performed ecclesiastical and other chores, following the lead given in Acts 6 where the Seven (not called deacons) serve tables and look after the widows so that the apostles can get on with the real work of preaching the word. How often have I heard clergymen at a conference say 'I'm still a deacon at heart' as they rush to get somebody else's breakfast for them. In reality, the deacon in the first four centuries was a very powerful person, confidant of the bishop, at his right hand at the altar and in the study, and the one most likely to succeed him. Between them, these ministers enabled the ministry of the ever-growing number of lay people, struggling with their identity in a world of much religious and racial confusion, and often cruelly attacked for their beliefs and for their refusal to take part in the social and religious habits of their friends and relations. The young churches needed strong leadership; and they also needed to stay together.

One of the most encouraging insights of the Second Vatican Council was to underline, in the scheme *De Ecclesia*, the importance of the local church. Emmanuel Lanne, commenting on this, writes that the local church provided that it is rightly ordered expresses in its life and activities the entirety of what it means to be the Church.[12] There is the bishop, there is the altar, there are the people gathered for worship, just as Ignatius describes them. As John Zizioulas has written, as quoted in a recent book on Eucharist and Church, the eucharistic assembly is a sign of the Church and in effect brings the Church into being in a visible way, and through the redeeming sacrifice there celebrated, enables the Church to fulfil its mission.[13] This is an ecclesiology which I personally warm to immensely. To begin with the local church and to see in it the entire ecclesial mystery (to use another phrase from Vatican II) enhances on the one hand the value of each and every episcopally ordered church and on the other hand gives the bishop his unique place. He is not the delegate of an archbishop or a Pope, he has a direct commission from Christ through the Church and he has the gifts of the Spirit appropriate to his order and responsibility. 'Be on your guard for yourselves and for all the flock over which the Holy Spirit has made you overseers (that is to say bishops)', says St Paul to the presbyter/bishops of Miletus, a belief which was to be reflected in all subsequent rites of ordination.

Such a theology might at first sight seem to argue for each local church being able to float free and declare unilateral independence as it sees fit. It might also argue for the rightness of a group of local churches breaking communion with the larger part of universal Christendom, and deciding to go *its* own way. Perhaps the Great Schism of 1054 was justified, and the eastern churches are well rid of the constraints of papacy and Roman canon law. Perhaps even it was right for the churches of the Reformation to separate from Rome, for the provinces of Canterbury and York to declare Rome in error and the reformed religion the way forward for Renaissance man and woman.

It is at this point, however, that St Paul and all the apostles would rise in a body and say 'God forbid'. For although it is important, on the one hand, to establish the ecclesial reality of churches that have separated from former associations (and that is why I currently believe that whatever Anglicanism and the Church of England may have done that is to be regretted or needs correction, we remain a communion of real churches, rightly ordered, proclaiming the entirety of the ecclesial mystery); on the other hand the importance of the local churches proclaiming the same faith, sharing communion with one another, admitting one another's members to communion, sharing ministries even and giving one another practical support – all this is in the very charter of the Church from its earliest days. Schism and separation of one church from another is and always has been invariably a tragedy and a disgrace. One of the reasons why I personally remain an Anglican is because we are actually repentant of our separation from other Christians and are doing our best to repair our many broken relationships. For from the earliest times, the unity and sense of identity of the local churches has been a first rather than a last thought.

The churches normally met one another in the person of their bishop. For several centuries, the bishop was invariably appointed from within the local church. He had learned the faith there, and was chosen because he could be relied on to keep the faith that the people would recognise. Athanasius, for example, when he became bishop of Alexandria 'was chosen by the vote of the whole people' and was declared 'lawfully appointed, not the man of contrary opinions but the man of the same faith'.[14] Rather as Eusebius of Caesarea, when he had represented his church at the Council of Nicea in 325, felt he had to write a letter to his home church to reassure them that the creed that had been put out at the Council represented a faith which was not substantially different from that enshrined in the creed of Caesarea.[15] For when we call the bishop the guardian of the faith, we are really saying that in his person and in his beliefs, he embodies the Christian convictions of the whole of his church, from the simplest and the most inarticulate, to the learned and prophetic. That is why controversial appointments of bishops with outspoken and apparently untraditional views cause such a stir and make the headlines.

Furthermore, the rites of ordination, properly understood, say similar and related things. In the early Church, a bishop, as we have seen in the case of Athanasius, has to be approved by the whole people. He was certainly not elected by majority vote, sometimes was pushed forward for ordination by popular acclaim (as in the case of

Ambrose and Augustine) but at the very least had to be presented to the people in order that they might declare him worthy (*axios*). By the fourth century, the ordination itself had to be performed by all the bishops of the province if able to be present, or by a minimum of three,[16] and it had to be specifically declared that the new bishop was the bishop of that particular city and none other. From the moment of his consecration onwards, to him would fall the responsibility of representing the whole of his local church in the wider councils of Christendom. He had therefore best know what his own church was thinking, worrying about, discovering even. As St Cyprian promised to his clergy at the beginning of his episcopate, he would 'do nothing without your advice and the consent of the people'.[17] When he went to meet other bishops, the people could be assured that it was their interests that he was representing.

What did the bishops talk about when they met? Fortunately for us, there has always been an extraordinary interest in bishops' meetings, with considerable care taken to record what they said and what they decided. The extensive records of provincial synods and ecumenical councils, of episcopal consultations and papal decrees contained in the collections of Mansi, Hardouin and Labbe may be a daunting prospect for the first-time enquirer. But we owe a great deal to these industrious editors for their scouring of the church historians and patristic authors, simply to tell us how often bishops met, either in full provincial synod or in smaller groups, such as the eighteen bishops who met at Ankara in 315, or on the grand scale in the ecumenical councils which were summoned and financed by emperors in the fourth and fifth centuries. They also record what was talked about, from debates about the day on which Easter was to be celebrated (as Eusebius relates in his account of the dispute between Pope Victor and the Asia Minor Christians living in Rome)[18] to the serious disruptions all over the Mediterranean world about the shock felt by Christians who had suffered personally and physically under the state persecution, at the lax treatment of Christians who had concealed their religious profession from the persecutors.[19] These compilers in turn depended on a long tradition of canon law collection. For a long time, records of meetings of provincial councils were kept privately in the diocesan offices of the presiding bishop or archbishop. Both the proceedings and the decisions were carefully written down by a scribe (*notarius*) and preserved for future reference. The decisions of ecumenical councils however had to be made available world-wide. So several copies of the acts were made on the spot, and given to bishops as they returned home. This is how the African bishops in 419 were able to compare the copy of the canons of the Council of Nicea which had come back to Carthage with Caecilian in 325, with the copies preserved on the one hand by Atticus at Constantinople and on the other hand by Cyril at Alexandria.[20] By the time of the Council of Chalcedon in 451, it appears that a body of episcopal decisions had been compiled, which included not only the doctrinal agreements and canonical legislation of Nicea I, Constantinople, Ephesus and Chalcedon, but also the canons of a group of contemporary and local councils – Ancyra and Neocaesarea (414, 415), Gangra, Antioch (341?) and Laodicea – some of whose canons seem to have been appealed to as representing decisions to be respected by all churches and not just to the provinces of their origin.[21] It was this kind of lumping together of more or less anything that looked like a canon and represented decisions coherent with the rest of the corpus that led canonists like Christopher Justel in the seventeenth century to believe that there already existed a universal code of canon law and episcopal decrees and decisions which was binding on the whole Church.[22]   Justel was heavily criticised by later canonists, notably by the Ballerini brothers from Verona.[23]

Nonetheless, that body of episcopal legislation to which Justel drew attention was eventually to form a major part of the earliest academic collections. On the one hand, for the east, there is the collection of John Scholasticus, i.e. John III, Patriarch of Constantinople (d.577) who made a massive collection of canons called the Synagogue, which he later enriched from the Novellae of the Emperor Justinian.[24] On the other hand in the west, we have the work of the sixth-century Scythian monk known as Dionysius Exiguus, who worked in Rome and has left us a substantial collection of canons in two editions, covering all four ecumenical councils, the five related fourth-century councils already referred to, the Canons of Sardica and the Canons of the many synods or councils held in North Africa.[25]   Dionysius' own edition was further modified in the eighth century when Pope Hadrian sent a copy to the Emperor Charlemagne (the edition known as the *Hadriana*).[26]   Dionysius may well have made use of the collected Nicene and Sardican canons (the *Vetus Romana*) which dates from the time of Julius I.[27] The collection ascribed to St Isidore, known as the *Hispana* or *Isidoriana* dates probably from between 419 and 451[28] and the version known as the *Prisca* also goes back to the fifth century.[29] Research into the manuscript history has revealed a variety of other traditions with important variations both in text and content, but this is a matter for the canonists and not for us who are looking at bishops in council. Suffice it to say, that an enormous amount of energy went into the recording and collecting of conciliar decisions and canonical legislation between the fourth and sixth centuries in particular, so that we are in fact remarkably well informed about episcopal ruminating at conferences and councils and can begin to see what their responsibilities were and how they responded to the challenge from the Church.

I have no need here to summarise the principal subjects for debate at the great ecumenical councils. The bishops had been summoned by the imperial authorities to seek the peace of the Church, divided as it was over opinions about the one God in Trinity and about the Person of the Redeemer. The debate took place, a form of words was agreed as representing the mind of the Church, this form was put out and the bishops were asked to sign. There was however no such thing as a vote. None of the decisions were majority decisions. Those who would not sign were either excommunicated or deprived of their sees. They might and indeed did come to life again in support of a schismatic section of the Church. But the council of bishops made decisions by consensus. Had they dared to think of anything like a two-thirds majority, they would have automatically invited a powerful schism.[30]

In the event, Eusebius of Nicomedia who voted against the Nicene decision, crawled back into favour with the emperor (since the Imperial Palace was at Nicomedia – in Church of England terms he would probably have been Dean of Windsor) and won many bishops over to his opinions. But there was never any question of the Church being a mixture of Arians and Catholics. Arians formed their own party, Catholics held their ground where they were; Arians removed Catholic bishops and Catholic bishops won back Arian dioceses. But Catholics like Basil of Caesarea in Cappadocia considered that whatever the deprivations suffered by his colleagues who supported the Nicene faith, he would communicate with them, even if they were in exile, but would studiously avoid communion with the Arianisers or any other heretical group.[31] When the Council of Constantinople reassembled, the bishops put out a new creed based, it is said, on the Creed of Jerusalem but substantiating the Nicene faith. But the decision at the end, once the proceedings had been agreed and the Imperial ratification obtained, was that any who did not accept the decisions of the council were to be deprived and only those who thus thought of the Trinity were to occupy the churches.[32] Drastic measures, we might conclude, but it certainly shows that when the bishops took counsel together in a formal assembly, they would not rest until a consensus agreement had been reached, with dire consequences for those who continued to oppose and clung to the beliefs of the heretics. Those who did not accept what the bishops decided were deprived of communion with them. Normally they regrouped and formed their own communion, some of these being very substantial, none more significant and long-lasting perhaps than the Monophysite or non-Chalcedonian churches of the eastern Mediterranean.

Harsh decisions perhaps in an even harsher world. But the full story has not yet been told. The bishops firmly believed that they were acting on behalf of the body of the faithful who had elected and appointed them and had asked them to act as their representatives. Having listened carefully to their own people, and having compared notes with their fellow bishops, being advised at the council itself by countless presbyters, deacons and acolytes (as Eusebius relates in the *Vita Constantini*), [33] they drafted and agreed a very careful account of what all might agree about the Christian experience of salvation and set this out in the most coherent language available for the Church at large to consider. They were in no hurry. They knew that there would be instinctive and immediate 'gut' reactions. Some would cheer, others would become very angry and set up furious opposition. No matter. Time would tell. Provided the bishops stood their ground, they would gather in to begin with those who were relieved at the cessation of Church divisions which had also divided society (as in North Africa the end of civil hostilities between Catholics and Donatists brought peace to both town and countryside). Then those who regrouped as an instinctive reaction to the decisions of the Council, reinforced by the Imperial authorities, would find opportunity to discuss within their own party ways both of making their own point and of seeking reconciliation with those from whom they had formerly separated.

The classic example of this is the 'homoiousian' party led by Basil of Ancyra, a group so nearly at theological agreement with the Nicene party and which was used to such effect by Basil of Caesarea and Hilary of Poitiers in the run-up to the Council of Constantinople, in the year 381. They made their stand; they were recognisable as a party. It was possible to enter into constructive dialogue with them. But what was so very vital in the first place was for the bishops representing catholic orthodoxy to say 'No'. Otherwise the homoiousion party could not have emerged as a group to do business with. The party objecting to the consensus of a council of bishops has to be identifiable; only then can the views of both parties be so refined as to enable progress towards an even better account of Christian truth than the Nicene Council had achieved in the year 325. [34]

And what of our current situation? The Church of England stands divided over the question of the ordination of women to the priesthood. In the House of Bishops of the General Synod, thirty-four voted in favour, nine voted against. In the Synod as a whole, very nearly one-third were opposed to the measure, and disquiet voiced in the parishes suggests that lay distress at the Synod's decision is considerable and not something that will quietly go away. The bishops who voted against are in a very difficult position. Each of them is now theologically unable to represent the conviction of his own diocese as to who may or may not officiate as a priest and gather the people of God together for the eucharist, the very heart of the life of any parish. The bishops opposed may refuse to ordain women to the priesthood; but there remains the even more serious question of the licensing and induction of a woman, ordained to the priesthood by a suffragan or neighbouring bishop, to have the sole pastoral care of a parish that has asked for her ministrations. Can a bishop at her induction commit her to a charge which, to quote the well known words, is 'your cure and mine', when in his own heart he does not believe that she has authority to carry out the duties of a priest? If he does so license her, he will be in danger of being seen as a Vicar of Bray. Sadly, the bishop is so often alone in such situations (particularly if he has no suffragan) and can be easily swung by other factors – the evident competence of the woman, the crying need of the parish and the happy partnership between prospective vicar and people that has been developing during the negotiating period.

In our present Church of England situation bishops opposed to the Measure seem to have extreme difficulty in standing together (like the semi-Arians) as a group to be identified, as a group to do business with. Straddled across dioceses which they cannot now totally represent, some talk about being agnostic about the ordination of women, others promise to value 'everyone's ministry', yet others say that in their diocese, the problem is so limited (six or seven women) that they can easily accommodate it; and others again treat each situation as it comes, and do their best to cope with the consciences of priests and parishes and individuals as each occurs. Standing together as a minority party within the House of Bishops is an unenviable option when on most issues, the bishops have to affirm solidarity and have been exhorted to 'stick together at all costs'. The bond between our bishops is understandably strong; and the lower clergy and the laity cannot expect access to their deliberations. But they (the bishops) do have to remember that while they affirm their solidarity and unity, others face the practical issues of being unable to communicate, unable to concelebrate, unable to rejoice in the communion of priesthood and Church community, simply because the unity of the ordained ministry which was appointed to serve the unity and growth of the Christian community, has been seriously jeopardised by the Synod decision of November, 1992. We have this awful sense of being left to sort things out for ourselves while our episcopal leaders, despite their arrangement for Provincial Episcopal Visitors, continue in unimpaired communion with their episcopal brethren, even though nine of them, and several suffragans in addition, firmly believe the November vote to have been a serious ecclesiastical error.

This is why it is important to take on board my analogy from the fourth century – the dialogue between the Catholic and the semi-Arian party, conducted by some of the most eminent and clear-minded theologians of the day, – then you will realise that I am not really speaking of a conflict in which one party will win, but of an attempt to move forward to a new situation, in which the insights of each party will at least be represented if not fully accommodated. But for this process to happen, there has to be to begin with (and I here use classic Hegelian/ Feuerbachian language) a thesis and an antithesis, two strongly opposed opinions, in order for a proper synthesis to be achieved. We need to hear the voice of the nine bishops opposed to the Measure. We need to hear the extent to which they are supported. We need to listen to the experience so far of Provincial Episcopal Visitors in dioceses where the Diocesan has little patience with those who cannot accept women as priests. We need to know where the battle lines are drawn; and then perhaps we can begin to open up a more constructive dialogue.

People speak sometimes glibly of reception. For some this means a patient waiting until the other side gives in – either the church will realise its mistake or the opponents of women priests will accept them with relief. But that is not how theology happens. Theology, like art, is a creative science, it looks at things as they are, it picks up insights and inspirations, it delves deep into tradition, and it peers earnestly into the future. And at the episcopal level, church leaders to begin with work carefully on what they individually and in their own church have received, then listen intently to what Christians in all walks of life and with all kinds of wisdom and spiritual experience are saying; they look outside their own church to take in what Christians of other cultures and other political experiences are able to contribute; and then they join with their fellow bishops to put their joint experience and discernment into a pool of knowledge, out of which they are then able, under the guidance of the Holy Spirit, to produce a generous-minded and pastorally-concerned assessment of the Church's faith and the Church's needs.[36]

But that is not the end of the story. The Church in all its members may react strongly and say 'That is not what we meant, you have considerably misunderstood us'. And if the Church says that, then the bishops must have the humility to accept that their voice is far from being the only one that counts and that the Holy Spirit has not simply spoken through them. The Councils of Ariminum and Seleucia, and probably that of Ephesus 449, were graced by bishops of considerable integrity who were absolutely assured that they had a God-given vocation to sort out the Church's divisions and to proclaim Christian truth. But the rest of Christendom said 'No'. As it did to the Eusebian party which called the tune for most of the reign of Constantine; as it did to the Anomoean party which dominated the reign of Constantius; as it did to the Donatist party which rivalled numerically at least the Catholic Church of North Africa in the time of St Augustine.

In our own time, so far as ordination of women to the priesthood is concerned, we are now in a period of reception. Some no doubt believe that this will be of comparatively short duration, that the opposition to women's ordination will weaken or that the opponents will leave for another church. Not enough serious consideration however has been given to the possibility that the Church of England may in the end as a body say 'No' to the Synod which passed the Measure in November 1992. When the North African Church in the third century struck out on its own with a policy of re-baptising those who had come in from heresy, it took seventy years for the church leaders of those provinces to change their policy and to reach agreement with the Roman Church. Other conciliar decisions have taken almost as long to be either accepted or rejected. Despite the large number of signatories at the Council of Nicea, 325, it took another fifty-six years until, after much division and debate, the churches as a whole found a way of affirming the essential truths declared at Nicea and of articulating these in a new *ekthesis*.[37] And where shall we be in the Church of England in fifty-six years' time or in seventy years' time for that matter? No doubt there is division and dissent ahead and the debate will continue, probably for many years. But the Church will one day be seen to have 'received' what the Spirit is saying in her life and history. And we can never presume that eventual 'reception' here means acceptance of the Synod's decision of 1992. It could mean quite the opposite.

There is one final matter which must be carefully reflected upon. Throughout Christian history, there has always been an understandable tendency to call the episcopal body to heel and to remind them that they are not an un-elected senatorial class who know what is best for the people, but persons appointed through the ministry of the whole Church, declared worthy, and admitted to office for their reliability and trustworthiness in representing the Church's faith, doctrine and manner of life. When, before the year 1969, in England, the bishops stood alone, presiding in the upper houses of the Convocations and responsible (under Parliament, it has to be admitted) for doctrine and discipline in the Church of England, they were bound in conscience to consider the entire spread of British Christianity, the whole scope of those who, churchgoing or not, considered themselves Christian in what seemed to be a Christian society. It was partly this sense of serving the whole of society and not just its churchgoing part that blocked the way for the 1928 proposed Book of Common Prayer.

Convocations and Church Assembly voted the proposed Book through; but it was Parliament which in fact did represent the people in the cities and the shires that cautioned against such a move and eventually voted it down. Church and society said 'No' but it paved the way for much more far-reaching liturgical reforms in the 1960s – reforms, it should be noted which in many ways parallelled liturgical changes in the western Church as a whole.

After 1969, with the creation of the General Synod which had powers 'to define doctrine', the bishops found themselves locked into (though not without privileges) a much more manageable group which could vote through decisions on matters of doctrine and discipline with a majority requiring only two-thirds of the vote. The model was frankly Parliamentary and automatically subject to being worked in a political way. A great deal depended on the election of candidates. There was of course no official party system and those elected were considered to be true representatives of the spread in churchmanship and opinions of the whole of the Church of England. Inevitably there are distinct groups in the Synod, and, what is perhaps more significant, when the candidates take to the hustings, they declare not only their interests but the line they will take on matters of current controversy. In the 1989 elections, for example, the vast majority of candidates made it quite clear which way they would vote on the matter of ordination of women to the priesthood. And this clearly had some bearing on the way in which they were elected or not elected as the case might be.

The result is a body which believes it has a mandate from the Church of England as a whole to make decisions on their behalf, much as a Government in power believes it has a right to do the same for the nation as a whole. They are not answerable to any other authority but Parliament. Appeals may be made in their debating to the wider authority of Scripture and tradition, and to the practices of other communions of churches which claim as we do to hold the one catholic and apostolic faith. But in the last resort, it is the vote of the Synod, endorsed by Parliament, which finalises the issue. The bishops have had the privilege on a matter of doctrine or discipline to design the way in which the issue is presented to the Synod. But even they do not have the final say. When the Synod votes, the Spirit is deemed to have spoken. The Synod thus becomes a governing body, a ruling junta almost, more prey to politics than to theology, swift to react to human rights and the spirit of the age, slow by virtue of its insularity to consider the consequence of its decisions for the wider Church of which it claims to be a part.

It was Vladimir Solovyov, friend of Dostoevsky, who warned that a body which believed itself to be the party of the people and held absolute powers during the time of its electoral rule, was the party most likely to defy the past and step out into new situations where it expected the people to follow. In *Crime and Punishment* this principle is driven to the brink of absurdity when Dostoevsky himself portrays a character who desperately tries to convince himself that though murder is wrong, in his case it was probably justifiable.[38] This is an extreme example; but it highlights the dangers of a ruling group believing that it has powers to make decisions contrary to tradition and custom, and then to expect those ruled to fall into line. That, I fear to expect those ruled to fall into line. That, I fear, is the expectancy from time to time of many an ecclesiastical governing power from the Vatican in Rome to the General Synod of the Church of England. The intention to lead the people and speak for the people may be good and right; but there are times when the foot-dragging of laity and lower clergy arouses impatience in those who have the whip hand. There is the sense aroused of 'We must move on, we can't wait'; and the decision is made. No ruling authority is blameless in this respect. It was the Emperor Constantine after all who wanted unity at a stroke and thought he had settled matters at the Council of Nicea, 325. But all he got was division and strife for the rest of his life. Synods and councils and curias should take note.

For church authorities to take the reins in so forceful a way can seriously disturb the balance that the conciliar movement of the early Church tried to uphold. The bishops in council were the servants of their local church, representing the people's faith. They were also the butt of the complaints of priests and people and had to take disturbances and doubts into the arena of their episcopal conference. At the council, they did their best, with considerable skill, they put agreements together and made recommendations about many practical matters about penance, marriage, brushes with paganism and diocesan boundaries. Their wisdom was imparted to the parishes; they knew it could be thrown back in their teeth and that they might have to start all over again. Which they did. But by and large they were content with this process. Episcopal dictators appear to have been few, and the church historians relish the telling of how some of these came to a sticky end (Paul of Samosata for example and George of Laodicea). But one cannot but help respect those bishops who gave all for the sake of their churches, who were prepared to reap the consequences of telling the truth, like St Athanasius and Hilary of Poitiers, preferring exile and loss of their episcopal home to compromising with the truth. One has the sense that these bishops lived under the truth, that there was a greater authority above them than their own opinion, to which they had to bow and to listen, that they had a concern to be in agreement with the world-wide Church and not just limit their decisions to what was expedient in their own province. It is striking in this respect to read the canons of the African Church and to note that where local matters were concerned, the bishops in council made their own decisions; but where the faith of the universal Church was concerned, there was always an appeal to what the other churches believed (for example, the canons of Nicea were sent for when they were discussing appeals over matters of discipline to overseas churches; and there was much correspondence with Rome over the visit of Pelagius' disciple, Caelestius).

We know what an impossible timetable most of our bishops have, and how many intractable situations and difficult clergymen they have to deal with. Their time for meeting in council is very limited. But one wishes in the Anglican communion at least that the bishops could behave and act in a traditionally conciliar way: that they would meet in council as needed or on a regular basis (as the Nicene canon says); that their deliberations and decisions at the universal level should be at the top of the agenda of provincial and local synods; and most of all that the bishops in council should feel the full weight of the tradition which they would be continuing. There would be the need to look back to the councils that have gone before and the decisions there made. There would be the need to reflect on the teaching and discipline of all the other episcopal churches. There would be the need to question if new developments proposed in council were a distortion of eternal truth or, as it should be, a new expression of this same truth for the modern world; and there would be the need for enormous patience, to wait and see how world-wide Christianity would respond to and if necessary reassess the insights they, the bishops, have reached in council.

Notes

1. Acts 14.23.
2. I Tim. 4.14.
3. B.J. Kidd, *A History of the Church to AD 461* (Oxford, 1922), vol.1, pp.379–382.
4. Bugenhagen, Letter to Christian III, in O. Vogt, *Dr Johannes Bugenhagens Briefwechsel* (Hildesheim 1966), p.156.
5. Christopher Laemmellius, *Historia Bugenhagiana* (Hasnia, 1706), p.81.
6. Acts 14.23, II Tim. 1.6.
7. I Clement 42.44.
8. (Oxford 1955), pp.224–226.
9. I Clement 42.44.
10. Ignatius, *Letter to the Trallians*, II.1 and III.1.

11. Joseph Bingham, *Antiquities of the Christian Church,* II.12.ff.
12. Emmanuel Lanne, 'The Local Church, its Catholicity and Apostolicity' in *One in Christ,* 1970-3, pp.288-313.
13. Paul McPartlan, *The Eucharist Makes the Church: Henri de Lubac and Jean Zizioulas in Dialogue* (Edinburgh, 1993).
14. Gregory Nazianzen, *Theological Oration,* 21.8.
15. Theodoret, *Ecclesiastical History,* I. 11.
16. Canon 4 of the Council of Nicea, 325.
17. Cyprian, *Epistola ad Presbyteros et Diaconos,* 5.4.
18. Eusebius, *Ecclesiastical History,* 5.23 ff.
19. As in the councils held at Carthage under Cyprian in 251, 252, 254, 255 and 256. Texts in Hardoin and Mansi.
20. See F. Maassen, *Geschichte der Quellen und Literatur des Canonischen Rechts im Abendland* (Gratz, 1870), pp.8-65.
21. This view was endorsed by the first canon of the Council of Chalcedon and confirmed in detail by the second canon of the Council of Trullo, AD 692.
22. C. Justel, *Codex canonum ecclesiae universae.*
23. In their edition of the works of Leo the Great, MPL 56.
24. See the edition of E. Schwartz, *Die Kanonsammlung von Johannes Scholastikos* Sitzungsberichte der bayerischen Akademie der Wissenschaften, Heft 6, 1933.
25. First edition, ed., A. Strewe (Berlin 1931); second edition in MPL 67.
26. See Maassen, op.cit., pp.441-471.
27. Referred to in the Council of Carthage of 419, according to which the canons of Nicea and Sardica formed a single document and were numbered serially.
28. MPL 84.
29. Preserved in two MSS - Vat Reg 1997 and Bod e Mus 100-2.
30. Careful records have been kept of episcopal signatures to the Nicene agreement. See C.H. Turner, *Ecclesiae Occidentalis Monumenta Iuris Antiquissima* (Oxford, 1913), Tom I. fasc II. pars I. Signatures were by province; and the geographical spread indicated by these signatures shows how universally Arius was condemned.
31. See Basil, *Letter* 89 to Meletius of Antioch.
32. Canons 6 and 7 of the Council of Constantinople I.
33. Eusebius, *Life of Constantine,* III.8.
34. On the Semi-Arians gathered around Basil of Ancyra, see H.M. Gwatkin, *Studies in Arianism* (2nd edition, Oxford, 1900).
36. See E.J. Yarnold and H. Chadwick, *Truth and Authority* (London 1977), pp.15-19.
37. i.e. at the first Council of Constantinople, AD 381.
38. Quoted in David MacDuff's translation of *Crime and Punishment* (Harmondsworth, 1991), p.12.

Ecclesiology and Communion

Robert Hannaford

Perry Butler's claim that the development of the Anglican Communion 'has ... been shaped more by historical circumstances than by deliberate design' betrays an idealist view of history but few would disagree with his conclusion that it 'is held together more by common loyalties than organizational structures'.[1] Since its emergence in the nineteenth and twentieth centuries as a world-wide Christian community the Anglican family of churches has typically described itself as a 'communion' of autonomous national churches. In various authoritative documents it has pointed to the shared experience of fellowship as the basis of its collective identity.[2] Unlike the confessional churches of the Reformation, or the Roman Catholic Church with its centralized hierarchical structure, Anglicans have been content to point to the fact of communion between their constituent churches and avoided justifying this too closely in terms of either doctrinal or ecclesiological principles. In this respect the Eames Commission's statement that Anglicans from provinces that do not ordain women to the episcopate are free to receive Holy Communion in provinces that do, and their assertion that this illustrates the 'fact' that they are still in communion, is typical and not consciously disingenuous.[3] Christians from other, more tightly defined, churches will no doubt claim that this is to put the cart before the ecclesial horse.

Anglicans, however, have by and large avoided identifying the grounds of their communion too tightly. The so-called Chicago or Lambeth Quadrilateral (adopted by the Anglican bishops of the United States of America in Chicago in 1886 and by the Lambeth Conference in 1888) is a case in point. The Quadrilateral identifies four essential marks of catholicity: the Holy Scriptures of the Old and New Testaments; the Apostles' and Nicene Creeds; the two dominical sacraments; and the historic episcopate.[4] This statement, based as it was on William Reed Huntington's identification of the 'absolutely

55

essential features of the Anglican position'[5] establishes Anglicanism
in a way that is open to a number of interpretations. Although, as Paul
Avis comments, this, like all appeals to 'fundamental articles', is
intentionally reductionist and minimalist it is also consistent with the
classic Anglican distinction between things necessary and things indifferent.[6] In identifying itself overwhelmingly in terms of the former
Anglicanism has chosen the way of inclusivism, requiring assent only
to what are regarded as the fundamental elements of faith.

This does not necessarily mean that Anglicanism is lacking in an
identity. Unlike churches that are identified by a clear confessional or
dogmatic structure Anglicanism can be characterized in terms of its
loose structure as a family of traditions. Anglican links are as much
familial and historical as doctrinal. Its identity consists not in an inner
core of doctrines concealed beneath its surface plurality but in the
family resemblance that obtains between its constituent traditions.[7]
This kind of identity is strong in the sense that it creates conditions
for Christians of diverse traditions to remain in communion with one
another. It is fragile in the sense that it depends not simply upon toler-
ance but upon constitutional arrangements – both implicit and explicit
– that permit and facilitate variant accounts of what it means to be
Anglican. This kind of identity remains feasible only for as long as
all Anglicans can continue to recognise their own Christian identity
within its loosely defined structures. The particular focus for the
present controversy about communion within Anglicanism lies in the
fact that many Anglicans believe that one of those basic structures –
the sacred ministry – has been called into question by the admission
of women to the priesthood.

The idea of 'communion' has therefore assumed a particularly important place in Anglican ecclesiology. Somewhat in advance of the
renaissance in thinking about this term throughout the Christian world it
was used by Anglicans as a designation for their own distinctive pan-
Anglican polity. Paradoxically while many contemporary scholars
would now see 'communion' as expressive of the very essence of ecclesial identity Anglicans have often appeared to use it in preference to the
term 'Church' when referring to their own ecclesial community (I was
recently corrected by a senior Anglican bishop when I referred to the
'Anglican Church'. 'There is no such thing' I was told, 'Only a communion of autonomous churches'). Although divisions within Anglicanism
now make it urgent, there has always been a need to keep the use of the
term communion under constant review. In what follows we will
consider recent developments in what is coming to be described as the
ecclesiology of *koinonia* and offer some concluding reflections on the
current predicament within Anglicanism.

I

The term 'communion', often simply transliterated in its Greek form *koinonia,* has become a key concept in recent ecumenical thinking. The statement *The Unity of the Church as Koinonia: Gift and Calling,*[8] issued following the Canberra assembly of the World Council of Churches in 1991, set the unity or *koinonia* of the Church in the wider context of the trinitarian God's purposes for the whole creation. In the opening paragraph the Church is described as a foretaste of God's plan 'to gather the whole of creation under the Lordship of Christ Jesus in whom, by the power of the Holy Spirit, all are brought into communion with God'. This line of enquiry was taken up and developed further at the fifth World Conference on Faith and Order at Santiago de Compostela in 1993.[9] The report of the Fifth Forum on Bilateral Conversations also noted that '*koinonia* is the fundamental understanding of the Church emerging from the bilateral dialogues' between different churches.[10] In the Joint Commission on Dialogue between the Roman Catholic Church and the Lutheran World Federation, for example, it forms the focus of a practical framework for union.[11] It has also played a key role in conversations between the Roman Catholic Church and the Anglican Communion culminating in the 1991 agreed statement *Church as Communion.* In this document the Second Anglican Roman Catholic International Commission (ARCIC II) responded to requests for clarification on the ecclesiological basis of its work, presenting a comprehensive reflection on *koinonia* as the central mystery of the Church's identity.[12]

Its use in modern ecumenical dialogue is also reflected in the wider field of ecclesiology with many wanting to argue, in the words of Pope John Paul II, that 'Communion is the very mystery of the Church'.[13] The first serious attempt to resurrect what J.M.R. Tillard has described as the ancient patristic vision of the Church as *koinonia*[14] occurred on the eve of the Second Vatican Council with the publication of Jerome Hamer's book *The Church is a Communion.* In this book, still couched in the language of traditional scholastic catholic theology, Hamer sees communion as expressive of the fundamental identity and inner cohesion of the Church.[15] Although rarely mentioned explicitly in the council documents Tillard insists that *koinonia* is 'the horizontal line around which the major ecclesiological affirmations of the Second Vatican Council revolve'.[16] Other recent works on ecclesiology which make significant use of the idea of communion include: Robert Kress's, *The Church: Communion, Sacrament, Communication,*[17] George H. Tavard's, *The Church, Community of Salvation,*[18] and *Christians in Communion* by the

Anglican theologian Paul Avis.[19] All are agreed in seeing communion/*koinonia* as synonymous with 'Church' and as a constitutive rather than a consequential feature of the Church's life and identity.

This view has not gone entirely unchallenged. In addition to reminding us that *koinonia* is a notoriously difficult term to translate – in the ancient Greco-Roman world it could mean 'having a share' in something, 'participation', 'fellowship', and even 'friendship' – John Reuman also points out that it is only a middle-level term in the New Testament, occurring a total of nineteen times, and that it is nowhere treated as synonymous with the term 'Church'.[20] On the face of it this seems to contradict the belief reflected in the bold assertion of ARCIC I that *koinonia* 'is the term that most aptly expresses the mystery underlying the various New Testament images of the Church'.[21] However, although the term might not have acquired the technical meaning now associated with it by the time of the writing of the New Testament, this does not mean that such a use is inconsistent with the biblical testimony. Rather than debating proof texts a more profitable line of enquiry would be to open up again the fundamental question of the nature of the Church. As we understand it the subject matter of ecclesiology is nothing less than the question of how the salvific will of God finds concrete expression in the community of men and women. Since the claim is that *koinonia* is the central mystery of the Church we can approach our enquiry, and at the same time test its veracity, by considering how far the term can be applied appropriately to the Christian experience of salvation. Before this question can be answered, however, we must examine the question of the nature of the God who makes salvation possible. Thus we shall attempt a cumulative uncovering of the ecclesiology of communion, situating it within the wider discussion of the salvific will of God for the whole creation.

II

Undoubtedly an important element in the recovery of the communion motif has been the recent revival of interest in trinitarian theology. Although it would probably be an exaggeration to say that these two developments coincide, they certainly overlap. Increasingly ecclesiological reflection has pointed to the correspondence between the visible communion of God's people and the trinitarian fellowship or *koinonia* of its life-giving divine source.[22]

Barth and Rahner both played key roles in the recovery of the trinitarian basis of all Christian theology with the former seeing it as an important implication of the central fact of divine revelation and the latter as the one mystery within the many mysteries of faith.[23] Both also stress absolute subjectivity as the starting point for discussion of the actualization of God in three distinct modes of existence (Barth) or in three distinct modes of subsistence (Rahner). This approach to the question of the divine unity within diversity has been criticised for failing to do justice to the dynamic nature of the God revealed in the history of salvation.[24] More recently a number of theologians have turned to the idea of communion or *koinonia* as a fruitful way of conceptualizing the trinitarian being of God. In his book *The Trinity and the Kingdom of God* Jürgen Moltmann develops a social and historical doctrine of the trinity. Significantly Moltmann begins his enquiry with the trinity of the divine persons and only then proceeds to discuss the unity. In doing so he sets out to reverse what he takes to be the traditional pattern of western trinitarian thinking and embraces boldly the idea that the one God is constituted as three individual divine persons. Moltmann argues that only a dynamic model of God as a communion of three persons protects the specifically Christian image of God and stops it from degenerating into simple monotheism.[25] The unity of God consists not in a static substance or essence but in the 'unifying-at-oneness' of the Father, Son and Holy Spirit revealed in the life, death and resurrection of Jesus.[26] Moreover the salvation-historical experience of God as trinity has its transcendental and primal ground in the inner-trinitarian life of God himself:

> The history of God's trinitarian relationships of fellowship corresponds to the eternal perichoresis of the trinity. For this trinitarian history is nothing other than the eternal perichoresis of Father, Son and Holy Spirit in their dispensation of salvation, which is to say in their opening of themselves for the reception and unification of the whole creation.[27]

In Moltmann *koinonia* is not simply a term for the Christian experience of fellowship; more importantly it encapsulates God's correspondence to himself in the Spirit-filled community of the Son.

Modern social theories of the trinity have a pedigree that extends back to the Hegelian Idealism of late nineteenth-century English, and particularly Anglican, theology. Theologians such as W. Richmond, J.R. Illingworth and R.C. Moberly developed a novel approach to the trinity, treating the Father, Son and Holy Spirit as a plurality of selves or persons in something like the modern sense of the term 'person', i.e., a distinct and separate centre of consciousness. J.R. Illingworth, for example, speaks of God as a 'society' on the grounds that 'if we are to think of God as personal at all, we must of necessity involve some kind of plurality in the conception; for personality implies this'.[28] This tradition was continued in the twentieth century by theologians such as Leonard Hodgson and Lionel Thornton. Thornton's work in particular draws very directly on the idea of *koinonia*. In his book *The Incarnate Lord* Thornton develops a view of the relationship between society and the individual which sets them both against the background of the new order revealed in Jesus' proclamation of the Kingdom of God. In such an order the individual is not defined over against society or *vice versa*. Rather 'the individual finds his vocation in terms of his function in society; and society achieves its destiny through identifying its corporate interests with the true vocational welfare of its individual members'.[29] It is this conception of spiritual plurality which is the correlative of spiritual unity that Thornton sees as providing the only authentic analogy from human society to the plurality of persons in the godhead.

Although Thornton has sometimes been accused of assimilating biblical teaching to the demands of philosophical thought there can be no denying that this was not his stated intention. Throughout the book in question he repeatedly insists that our knowledge of the trinitarian nature of God is entirely dependent upon revelation.[30] Significantly Thornton sees this revelation as founded not only upon the teaching of Jesus[31] but also upon the experience of the New Testament Christian community. It is the new order of fellowship experienced in the Church that raises the question of divine *koinonia*.[32] The experience of renewed human *koinonia* in the Church enables us to recognize its transcendent source in the *koinonia* of God himself:

> Since the new law of *agape* flows down into the new community through the Spirit of Christ from the 'Father of Our Lord Jesus Christ', this law of *agape*, revealed in the Messiah's life story and reproduced in the Spirit as the inner principle of life in the New Order, must be referred back to its transcendent source in the life of God.[33]

However, Thornton also posits a second stage of reflection because he insists that the revelation once given 'throws light upon the whole structure of the universe and of history as apprehended by man through successive domains of experience'.[34]

This second movement – reflecting upon the nature of created human experience in the light of trinitarian doctrine – has become a significant feature of modern trinitarian theology. In his book *Trinity and Society* Leonardo Boff, for example, has taken the term *koinonia* as a key motif for understanding the unity of God but, more importantly, he sees it as indicative of 'the relevance of the Trinity to our desire for a society that lives together in more open communion,

equality and respectful acceptance of differences'.[35] In the same vein
the members of the British Council of Churches Study Commission
on Trinitarian Doctrine Today produced a report which concentrated
mainly on drawing out the implications of trinitarian belief for the
Christian understanding of creation and salvation. So, for example, the
report claims that a firmer grasp of trinitarian thinking can lead to a
deeper understanding of what it means to be a person since 'the fulfilment of human beings is to be found in relationships in community
and not in self-assertive individualism'.[36] More ambitiously Professor
Colin Gunton, a member of the Commission, set out to construct a
'trinitarian ontology' as the foundation for a renewed doctrine of
creation in his recent Bampton Lectures 'The One, The Three and
The Many'.[37] Sociality or being in relation has often been regarded
as a secondary or consequential feature of the inner trinitarian life of
God. Gunton sees this as a fundamental misconception of the relational ontology of trinitarian being and calls for a revision in our
understanding of sociality. Although a conceptual distinction can be
drawn between being and relation this is not reflected in the ontological order of the godhead. On the contrary 'the persons do not simply
enter into relations with one another but are constituted by one another
in the relations'.[38] Gunton here echoes the words of John Zizioulas
when he states that the being of God is not a bare unity but a being
in communion and that we have to do here with a new ontology of
communion.[39]

In keeping with his overall project Gunton then proceeds to draw
analogies between the being in relation of God and the being in
community of the created human order. The complexities of Gunton's
discussion need not detain us here but it is pertinent to note the role
that he assigns to ecclesiology. Ecclesiology enters the discussion at
two levels, both of which Gunton regards as decisive for our understanding of the human condition: first, because the Christian vision
of renewed community presupposes atonement or the healing of relationships;[40] secondly, and more generally, because he sees
ecclesiology as having a direct bearing upon the Christian doctrine of
creation. At this second level, according to Gunton, ecclesiology is
'in the general sense of the word ... the basis of human being'.[41] It
is the embodiment of social being in the *koinonia* of a true *ecclesia*
that constitutes the fullest expression of the created potential of human
reality.[42] Gunton does not address the question of the relationship
between these two levels of ecclesiology, of how the vision of a
renewed human *koinonia* is actually mediated through the historic
Christian community. Gunton's reference to trinitarian embodiment in
a 'true' *ecclesia*, suggesting as it does that the trinity is an idea to

which the Church must conform, illustrates the problem. The subject matter of ecclesiology is not human potential in the abstract but the particular manifestation of God's salvific will for the whole of creation in the human community of those whom Christ has made his own. It is precisely within this community, and not within an idealized *ecclesia*, that *koinonia* is embodied. As we shall see in a moment, the hesitation we have about Professor Gunton's general project arises from his failure to situate trinitarian reflection in the context of the Church's concrete encounter with Christ.

Gunton's work represents a further refinement in the two-fold movement of trinitarian reflection that we noted in Thornton. Gunton acknowledges the grounding of our knowledge of God as trinity in the economy of salvation but he insists that this does not preclude an exploration of what the trinitarian being of God allows us to say about the world. It is quite clear that his principal concern is to draw analogies from the being of God to the world.[43] So, for example, Gunton sees human community as an analogue of the divine trinitarian community. We need to be cautious about this way of approaching trinitarian theology. The terms used by believers to describe God are already analogies drawn from our experience of the created order. The claim that the concepts so applied can then in turn be used to speak analogically about the world ought to be treated with reserve. At a deeper level there must also be doubts about whether or not Gunton's approach is consistent with the radical particularity of the Christian doctrine of God. Rowan Williams warns against an approach to God that simply projects onto him what we cannot achieve, namely, 'a systematic vision of the world as a necessarily inter-related whole'.[44] Such a God can all too easily represent a retreat from the tragic dimension of human life. In the face of such totalization Christian faith unashamedly points to the story of Jesus as the ground and limit of what can be said of God. Indeed it is precisely the question of how the particularity of Jesus of Nazareth can be a specific mode of the infinite that characterizes trinitarian theology. In the pathos of the cross God's otherness is seen to include and not to exclude the discontinuities of human life and thus to resist the false irony of systemization. Whether reflection upon the world in the light of the trinity is legitimate remains to be seen but it cannot be set in hand by categorizing and projecting onto the infinite our own refusal to come to terms with the particularity of human experience.

Lewis Ayres has pointed out that there is an appropriate and necessary order for reflection on the trinity.[45] This seems to be the point behind Karl Rahner's famous statement that the economic and immanent trinity are identical.[46] Traditionally a distinction has been drawn between the discussion of God as he is in himself (the immanent or essential trinity) and God as he is revealed in creation and redemption (the economic trinity). Rahner insists that this does not reflect the order of Christian experience and the grounding of the knowledge of God in the economy of salvation. Putting it very crudely, the Christian community developed a view of the nature of God that was consonant with its experience of life in Christ. A trinitarian account of the being of God is, as it were, the necessary implication of the salvific story of Jesus. Does this mean that the immanent trinity is no more than a human construction, a postulate derived from human experience? Donald MacKinnon's image of 'transcription' is helpful here.[47] Although Christian experience begins with the particulars of Jesus' life and death, these do not make sense unless we subsequently come to know them as 'derivative, transposed from what is prior'.[48] God's self-limitation, his being other than himself in Jesus, cannot be understood unless we see it as a *transcription* into time of his eternal being-other-than-himself as trinity.

Rahner's dictum should thus be read as a statement of the theo-logic implicit in the basic Christian conviction that 'God was in Christ reconciling the world to himself'. In reconciling the world to himself God declares who he is and this establishes the pattern for Christian theological reflection. We might say then that for Christian theology there is a grammatical link between the theology of salvation and the doctrine of God. Echoing this and commenting on 1 John 4.8 Walter Kasper states that 'The revelational statement "God is love" is ... at the same time a statement about the being of God and, as such, a statement about salvation'.[49] Only because God is in himself the loving community of Father, Son and Holy Spirit can we speak of him revealing himself to us as love. It follows that statements about our experience of the love of God in Christ must be equivalent in some sense to statements about God himself.

Drawing these threads together it is now possible to be a little more precise about the order and pattern of theological reflection and also return in the process to our main concern, the Church and the *koinonia* of the godhead. If the trinitarian nature of God emerges from and secures our understanding of salvation then it follows that all talk of God must be grounded in Christology and hence in the Christian community's engagement with Christ. Paradoxically this must also be true of what we say about the immanent or essential trinity. While belief in the immanent trinity is a necessary correlative to the belief that God is constitutive of what is significant in the life of Jesus, this cannot be established separately from our engagement with the particularities of that life. The theo-logic that we have outlined suggests that we cannot divorce our consideration of God's eternal being from the process of trying to come to terms with the pathos of Christ's life and death. Not only do we learn that God can be other-than-himself in Christ but, in the desolation of the cross, we learn that God can be just 'other' and hence hidden and unknown. God's immanence is not, therefore, a mere postulate of salvation but a feature of his capacity to be concealed from himself in Jesus' agony.

The understanding of Christ cannot, however, be divorced from consideration of the new community that emerged in response to his life and ministry. It is self-evidently the case, as many New Testament scholars insist, that it is impossible to detach the historical Jesus from the New Testament Church's perception of him. We cannot tell the story of Jesus without also telling the story of the infant Church. The desire for such a detachment is, however, misplaced. The significance of Jesus lies precisely in the new life revealed in the Christian community.[50] Christology is critical reflection on the person of the New Adam and his story is incomplete unless he is seen as the 'first of many brethren'. Jesus' identity is revealed in those who come after and their engagement with him. Seeing Jesus, and thus the God who is constitutive of his life, involves entering into the new pattern of relationships inaugurated by the preaching of the gospel. Coming to know the God of Jesus Christ means entering into the community whose life is not simply an echo of his ministry but is integral to his identity as saviour. In other words, as the primary datum for theological reflection on the trinitarian being of God, Jesus' life is inseparable from the Church which is both the fruit and the historical embodiment of his salvific reality.

Our lengthy excursus on trinitarian theology highlights the key role that reflection on the mystery of the Church plays in the establishment of a specifically Christian doctrine of God. All talk about the trinity has to take God's revelation of himself in the life, death and resurrection of Jesus as its point of departure. This begins but does not end with the historical life of Jesus, for if it did we would be left simply with a new teaching about God. Ecclesiology completes the discussion of Christology by showing how in the new community of the Church God's revelation is also an impartation of himself. Indeed God reveals himself precisely by imparting himself in the healed relationships of the new community, and it is this that compels us to speak of him as Father, Son and Holy Spirit. God imparts himself by incorporating men and women into the *koinonia* of his Kingdom. The Church as the historical manifestation of that Kingdom is thus internal and not external to the revelation of God as trinity. John Zizioulas reflects this when he describes the Church as 'the image of the Triune

God'.[51] It would be idolatrous, of course, to describe the Church in such terms if it were seen as having only a secondary or consequential relation to the primary acts of revelation. The Church is an image of the trinity not because it bears some likeness to the divine nature but because its *koinonia* is integral to the divine *economia* of salvation and grace.

III

The link between talk of the trinity and ecclesiology lies in *koinonia* which is seen to be both the divine basis and the end of the Christian vision of salvation. In the new community of the Church God's impartation of himself is revealed as the *koinonia* of the Kingdom. The end of all things is not the perfection and perpetuation of individual existence but their reconciliation in God. As Colin Gunton puts it, 'human community becomes concrete in the Church, whose calling is to be the medium and realization of communion: with God in the first instance, and with other people in the second, and as a result of the first'.[52] Moreover, the divine impartation of *koinonia* in the economy of salvation is seen to have its ultimate foundation in the eternal intra-trinitarian impartation of the Father's divinity in the Son and the Holy Spirit.

The central New Testament images of salvation are those that refer to incorporation into Christ: salvation as a union with the life and death of Christ. The Pauline corpus describes this in terms of being 'in Christ' or 'in the Lord' or 'in Jesus Christ'. Mystical interpretations of these references, with their connotations of individual – one might say private – perfectibility, fail to do justice to Paul's communion-based model of salvation and are inconsistent with other elements in his theology. Paul's frequent references to the metaphor of the body and its members suggests that he understood salvation in relational terms. He links union in Christ with union or *koinonia* in the Church. Indeed these are not separable in the mind of Paul. This is no more strongly evident than in Paul's references to baptism. In Galatians he speaks of baptism into Christ and of the baptised having 'put on' Christ (Gal. 3.27). Again in Romans he speaks of baptism into the death of Christ (Rom. 6.3). It is by sacramental washing with water that the faithful are grafted into Christ and come to share in his death and resurrection. Parallelling these references to union with Christ Paul also speaks of baptism 'into one body' (1 Cor. 12.13). In Paul's theology to be 'in Christ' is to be in 'the body of Christ'. This is one reality and not two. It is by incorporation into the Church that men and women are made incorporate in Christ. As the late Bishop John Robinson put it,

> The Christian because he is in the Church and united with him in the sacraments, is part of Christ's body so literally that all that happened in and through that body in the flesh can be repeated in and through him now.[53]

The *koinonia* of the Church is not, however, an end in itself for it serves the mystery of God's will (Eph. 1.9), his plan to restore the broken unity of the universe (Eph. 1.10). The Church, which holds within itself 'the fullness of him who himself receives the entire fullness of God', is a public sign and manifestation of God's eternal decree of salvation for the whole creation (Eph. 1.23). Although not prominent in the New Testament the early Church's confession of Christ as mediator in God's act of creation and as Lord over nature has a direct bearing upon our enquiry. In 1 Corinthians 8.6, for example, we read, '... there is one God, the Father, from whom are all things, and for whom we exist, and one Lord, Jesus Christ, through whom are all things, and through whom we exist'.[54] Passages such as this, which speak of the pre-existence of Christ, obviously present particular problems of interpretation.[55] As Walter Kasper points out, they cannot be understood unless they are linked with the early Church's confession of faith in Christ as the one in whom God's plan of salvation reaches its fulfilment. It is because the Church saw Christ as the end of salvation that it also saw him as 'the final definition of the world and man'.[56] Christ is seen as the mediator of creation because it is in him that God reveals the universal perspective of his salvific will. In other words references to the mediatorship of Christ in creation are soteriological in import, representing a universalization of the saving work of Christ. This link is particularly clear in the New Testament references to Christ as cosmic redeemer. Take, for example, the following passage from Colossians:

> He is the image of the invisible God, the first born of all creation; for in him all things were created, in heaven and on earth, visible and invisible, whether thrones or dominions or principalities or authorities – all things were created through him and for him. He is before all things, and in him all things hold together. He is the head of the body, the Church; he is the beginning, the first-born from the dead, that in everything he might be pre-eminent. For in him all the fullness of God was pleased to dwell, and through him to reconcile to himself all things, whether on earth or in heaven, making peace by the blood of his cross. (Col. 1.15-20; cf. Eph. 1.1-22)

The reference to Christ as first-born of all creation presupposes the final reference to Christ as the universal redeemer. Christ is seen as the ground of unity in creation – the one in whom all things hold together – because he is the one in whom God is reconciling all things to himself. Christ is celebrated as the one in whom all things were created because he is confessed as the eschatologically definitive sign of salvation. Creation is viewed in the light of its renewal in Christ. Although Paul does not use the term *koinonia* in this passage, the reality to which it refers is clearly in his mind. Salvation is understood as the union or reconciliation of all things in God and this is read back into the understanding of creation itself. The world which Christ is reconciling to the Father is already held together in him. *Koinonia* is the substance not only of the salvation from sin and death but is also revealed thereby as the goal of the first salvation from nothingness.

It is significant to note that Paul's celebration of Christ as cosmic redeemer sets the Church within the broadest perspectives of the history of salvation. It is the Church, of which Christ is head, that is the first-fruits of God's plan to reconcile all things to himself. The Christian community's mission is to bear witness to God's eternal plan to bring all things into 'a unity in Christ' (Eph. 1.10). Moreover, incorporate in Christ and sealed by the Holy Spirit, the Church is not only herald of this gospel but also a visible sign and pledge of the heritage that awaits the whole creation (Eph. 1.13f).

The *koinonia* of the Church points beyond itself to the promised reconciliation of all things in God. Fr Congreve, an early member of the Society of St John the Evangelist, an Anglican religious community founded in the nineteenth century by Fr R.M. Benson, writes powerfully about the Christian vision of the unity of all creation in his treatment of the doctrine of the Church and the communion of saints:

> The first result of this descent of the Holy Spirit at Pentecost was the creation of this new mystery, the restoration of the broken unity of mankind in Christ. 'There is neither Greek nor Jew, bond nor free, male nor female: for ye are all one in Christ Jesus.' This was the gospel of St Paul, the ministry of which filled his apostolate with wonder and joy – the gathering together of all races in Christ, the inauguration of the Communion of Saints in the Church of Christ by the power of the Holy Spirit.[57]

Communion is not simply a means to an end; it is the substance of the Christian hope of salvation for the whole creation. As the body of Christ, who is himself the first born from the dead, the Church is

the world viewed from its end. In its fellowship the Church anticipates the final reconciliation of all things.

IV

As Colin Gunton suggests, it is in the incipient trinitarianism of the
Fourth Gospel that the link between the *koinonia* of the godhead and
that of the Church is at its clearest.[58] In the High Priestly prayer of
Jesus, for example, the fellowship or communion of believers is said
to have its ground in the relationship between the Father and the Son:

> I do not pray for these only, but also for those who believe in me
> through their word, that they may all be one; even as thou, Father,
> art in me, and I in thee, that they also may be in us, so that the
> world may believe that thou hast sent me. The glory which thou
> hast given me I have given to them, that they may be one even as
> we are one, I in them and thou in me, that they may become
> perfectly one, so that the world may know that thou hast sent me
> and hast loved them even as thou hast loved me. (John 17. 20-23)

Many have taken this passage as warrant for preferring an ontological account of the nature of the Church. In their major study of
ecclesiology the Anglican theologians Anthony and Richard Hanson,
for example, dismiss the question 'What is the Church for?' as inap-
propriately utilitarian and mechanistic.[59] Their claim is that one can
only ask what the Church is, not what it is for. The Johannine vision
of communion suggests no such sharp polarization between questions
of function or purpose and being or nature. It is certainly clear that
John lays enormous stress on the unity of the Church and in that sense
on its structure and form. The Church's being as a *koinonia* is said
to reflect the unity of the Son and the Father. However, against the
view that would stress the Church's being to the exclusion of its
mission or function comes the corrective that communion has a
purpose, namely 'that the world may believe'. Communion relates both
to the being and the mission of the Church. The Church is constituted
as a communion whose mission it is to proclaim the saving work of
Christ in drawing all things into fellowship or communion with the
Father.

There is a tendency to focus on the ontological understanding of the
Church   in   the   current   discussion   about   communion   within
Anglicanism. In particular many of those who regard the ordination
of women to the priesthood and episcopate as a departure from apostolic tradition have claimed that they are no longer in communion with

their fellow Anglicans. Being in communion, they would argue, is a matter of all or nothing. We shall give further discussion to the current Anglican predicament in the final section of this paper; for the moment we should note that this particular reading of the situation gives complete priority to the ontological dimension of *koinonia*. As we have suggested, such an approach fails to do justice to the dynamic character of ecclesial *koinonia*. John understands communion as both the gift and the task of the Church. The communion of Christians with one another is the gift of the Father through the Son but it is also Jesus' prayer that 'they all may be perfectly one'.

The tendency to polarise the discussion of communion so that it is seen either in terms of ontology or in terms of the mission and task of the Church arises in part from a failure to note its eschatological character. Jesus' prayer, quoted above, continues as follows:

Father, I desire that they also, whom thou hast given me, may be with me where I am, to behold my glory which thou hast given me in thy love for me before the foundation of the world (John 17.24).

Koinonia is already Christ's saving gift to the Church but it is such as an anticipation of the glory that will be his final gift. While time remains – and as those who already share in the first fruits of salvation – the Church is called to seek an ever closer conformity to the unity that obtains between the Father and the Son. As a manifestation of the eschatologically decisive saving action of God the Church's communion is both a present reality and a hope for the future. It is this which makes communion both the gift and the calling of the Christian community. The Church is called, paradoxically, to an ever more perfect realization of what it already is. Alongside that *koinonia* which is constitutive of the Church's identity we must also speak of a corresponding discipleship of *koinonia*. As those who live by the Spirit who draws men and women into the fellowship of the one God, Christians are also called to walk by the same Spirit (Gal. 5.25; cf. Col. 2.6).[60]

Salvation understood as *koinonia* is the ground and the goal of the Church's life. In its discussion of the ecclesiology of communion the second Anglican Roman Catholic International Commission (ARCIC II) described the Church as a 'mystery' or 'sacrament'.[61] In explaining this the commission describes the Church as 'a visible sign which both points to and embodies our communion with God and with one another; as an instrument through which God effects this communion; and as a foretaste of the fullness of communion to be consummated when Christ is all in all'.[62] The sacramental model points up the fact that the Church has its existence beyond itself in relation to both Christ and the world.

The hesitation felt by some about this approach to the theology of the Church arises no doubt from a fear of misplaced triumphalism. However, catholic scholars are generally agreed in seeing the term 'sacrament' as applying primarily to Christ himself and only derivatively to the Church. Karl Rahner, who early on described the Church as the 'primal' or 'fundamental' sacrament,[63] later acknowledged the misleading nature of this terminology.[64] Moreover, Henri de Lubac's famous definition acknowledges that Christ himself is the primary sacrament of God's eschatological mercy:

> If Christ is the sacrament of God, the Church is for us the sacrament of Christ; she represents him, in the full and ancient meaning of the term, she really makes him present. She not only carries on his work, but she is his very continuation, in a sense far more real than that in which it can be said that an human institution is its founder's continuation.[65]

The sacramental model, while stressing the unity that exists between Christ and the Church, is also thoroughly consistent with his Lordship over it. The Church is only sacrament because Christ himself is the primary sacrament of God's love and mercy. Moreover, although the model makes strong claims about the unique salvific significance of the Church it also draws attention to the Church's existence as a sign and instrument of God in the world. The pastoral orientation of the Church towards the world is evident in the references to the sacramental model in *Lumen Gentium*, the Dogmatic Constitution on the Church of the Second Vatican Council. In its pages great stress is laid upon the Church as a sign of God's plan for the restoration of the unity of all humankind and it is this that led the council fathers to describe the Church as a sacrament.[66] Similar thinking is reflected in Pope John Paul II's recent encyclical on commitment to ecumenism. Quoting from a letter addressed to his fellow bishops he describes the Church as the 'inseparable sacrament of unity':

> The Church is not a reality closed in on herself. Rather, she is permanently open to missionary and ecumenical endeavour, for she is sent to the world to announce and witness, to make present and spread the mystery of communion which is essential to her, and to gather all people and all things into Christ.[67]

The Church is a visible sign, embodying human communion with God and with others. So far from being triumphalist the sacramental model is particularly suited to a pastoral and mission-oriented understanding of the nature of the Church.

Our main purpose in raising the question of a sacramental model is, however, to consider how this insight about the eschatological nature of salvation-*koinonia* relates to our understanding of the Church and its mission. Here we should note immediately that sacramental language presents us with an appropriate vehicle for uncovering the dynamic character of ecclesial *koinonia*. Alongside the dialectic of gift and task we can now place what might be termed the double character of sacramental signs.[68] A sacrament is never a self-contained reality. It is structured both by its relation to created reality and its relation to the new order of salvation and redemption in Christ. This is what gives it the capacity to be both a symbol of human hope and a sign and embodiment of the promised fulfilment of *koinonia*. 'Signs' gain their meaning by pointing beyond themselves. They operate by rules or conventions that determine their referential context. Discovering what they signify means entering into their mode of signification. In the case of the Church the reality signified is God's kingdom of reconciliation and so the referential context is determined by faith. Or, as Origen says, the spiritual meaning of a *mysterium* or a holy sign can only be discovered when we live the mystery. The Church becomes a sign and instrument of salvation when men and women discover it as the communal and liturgical context for the celebration of God's saving action in Christ. Coming to see this, however, also involves embracing the historical and social nature of the sign. Indeed, one might say that this is precisely the test of faith involved in discerning the mystery. To enter into the referential context of this sign is to see it as a human community of hope whose life is already an anticipation of God's kingdom.

It is important to stress then that the Church is simultaneously a human society and an embodiment of the promised fullness of communion and it is this that constitutes its double character as a sacrament. Paradoxically, although the Church points to the reality of salvation, as a human society it also reflects the hope and therefore the need for salvation. It is a community of hope and celebration, of discipleship as well as joy. Over the centuries Christians have been tempted to ignore the double character of the Church, preferring to locate its true significance in what lies hidden from view. In doing so they have ignored the symmetry that exists between the sociality of the Church's empirical form and that of its eschatological significate, God's kingdom of reconciliation and peace. In empirical terms the Church has the form of a human society, albeit a fairly heterogeneous one, but, united with Christ, it can become in the event of faith a sign and foretaste of human incorporation into the sociality of the divine *koinonia*. This two-fold orientation of the Church, in the one direction towards humanity and hence the yearning of men and women for genuine community and in the other towards God and his kingdom characterizes the Church at every level of its existence. Articulating this is, of course, one of the most intractable problems in ecclesiology.

The double orientation of the Church has sometimes been conceptualized by drawing a distinction between the Church as a visible, public, structure and as an invisible reality of grace. This can all too easily lead to an ecclesiological monophysitism, where the human and divine elements are sharply polarised, with the former becoming ultimately irrelevant. The human or public face of the Church is a necessary and not a contingent feature of its sacramentality. It is constituted as a sign precisely because there is a symmetry between its empirical form and the eschatological mystery to which it points. It is in the visible *koinonia* of the Church that the divine *koinonia* of God's kingdom is made manifest. As Edward Schillebeeckx writes in his important study of sacramental ecclesiology:

> The Church is a visible communion in grace... The inward communion in grace with God in Christ becomes visible in and is realised through the outward social sign... It was the custom in the past to distinguish between the soul of the Church (this would be the inward communion in grace with Christ) and the body of the Church (the visible society with its members and its authority). Only too rightly, this view has been abandoned... The visible Church itself is the Lord's mystical body. The Church is the visible expression of Christ's grace and redemption, realized in the form of a society which is a sign (*societas signum*).[69]

Locating what is ultimately significant about the Church in what lies beneath the surface of its public and human face is ultimately destructive of the very idea of the Church itself. As a sacrament the Church is necessarily a human sign of the bestowal of divine grace.

The attempt to draw a distinction between a visible and an invisible Church is a particular response to the eschatological nature of its foundation. Quite understandably there is a desire to underwrite the divine as well as the human dimension of the Church. As a community founded upon that which is final and ultimate there must be an important sense in which the Church points beyond itself. The difficulty with the visible/invisible divide is that it is a solution to this challenge which polarises the human and divine in the Church and does not demonstrate how, without confusion, they jointly constitute the Church. John Zizioulas offers an interesting and unusual approach to this problem. The recent rediscovery of the eschatological character of the Church has led some theologians either to describe the

Church as existing in the time between the resurrection of Jesus and the *eschaton* or to speak of the *eschaton* as somehow continuously present in the time of the Church. Zizioulas sees both approaches as inconsistent with the transcendence or ultimacy of the *eschaton*. To suggest that the *eschaton* can be present permanently in the Church, even in a sharply attenuated form, appears inconsistent with the freedom and sovereignty of God. God cannot be enclosed in history. Nonetheless Zizioulas is quite clear that in the Eucharist the Church anticipates the *eschaton*. Indeed, so strong is his sense of presence at this point that Zizioulas sees 'no room for the slightest distinction between the worshipping eucharistic community on earth and the actual worship in front of God's throne'.[70] However, this presence is not permanent but momentary. Zizioulas conceives the eucharistic identification of the Church on earth with the community of heaven rhythmically or eschatologically rather than ontologically. This is not a permanent presence, only a continual 'visitation' in which the Church moves from foretaste to foretaste, constantly acquiring that which is also lost again and again. Zizioulas' resistance to the idea of a permanent embodiment of the *eschaton* in the life of the Church is well placed. This can all too easily lead to the *eschaton* being seen as little more than the result or outcome of the historical life of the Church. The *eschaton* is not a presence *within* history but a presence from *beyond* it. Insofar as the Church is a human institution it exists within the flow of human history. However, as a eucharistic community the Church owes its existence entirely to the future. In this sense the kingdom of the end times does not abide in the Church from the past – as if it were an inevitable outcome of the incarnation – but rather breaks into its life from the future. The Church exists epicletically, being constantly constituted by the Spirit who does not so much abide in it as visit it from beyond history. The rejection of eschatological inevitabilism as a solution to the double orientation of the Church leads Zizioulas to dismiss all appeals to the past in securing its identity under God: 'There is no security for her to be found in any historical guarantee as such – be it ministry or word or sacrament or even the historical Christ himself. Her constant dependence on the Spirit proves that her history is to be constantly eschatological'.[71] Zizioulas is right to reject the notion of a permanent presence as representing a collapse into time of the ultimacy and distinctiveness of God's kingdom. However, does he not in his idea of momentary visitation open himself to the same criticism? If in the Eucharist the Christian community is absolutely identified with the *eschaton*, even in such a way that this presence is then lost, should we not say that this too is a point at which the age to come is absorbed into time?

The suspicion must be that Zizioulas has himself polarised the double character of the Church – what we have also termed its human and divine natures – and that his notion of eschatological visitation, like the rejected distinction between the visible and invisible Church, represents nothing less than a collapse of the Church into one pole at the point of visitation.

The difficulty with Zizioulas' view is that it appears incapable of accounting for the fact that the Church as sign is jointly constituted by its orientation to the community of men and women and to the new *koinonia* of the age to come. The Church is a sign of the coming kingdom but it is always such as a community of those who in a sense yearn for what they already have in their midst. Self-evidently the Church is a community of yearning and expectation but it is also a community that already tastes the first fruits of salvation. The problem comes whenever we polarise this double orientation and then try to identify one pole or other with particular aspects of the life of the Church. Its eschatological ordering means neither that it is a community constantly frustrated by a vision of glory that is just out of reach nor that it is in a position to celebrate a perfection that it patently lacks but rather that its life at every point is characterized by both *promise* and *fulfilment*. We choose these terms because they seem particularly suited to express the Church's origin from the end. In saying that the Church is constituted jointly by its orientation towards the natural human community and the community of the age to come we are not suggesting that its grace-full power as a sacramental sign is in anyway humanly constructed. The Church is not constituted by the age-long yearning of human beings for perfection but by the call of God himself. The Church exists because of new relationships created as a consequence of the death and resurrection of Jesus. This new community, however, represents not the obliteration of human yearning but its transformation and fulfilment. In Christ we discover the true substance of human hope and longing. The kingdom is God's but it comes to fulfil and complete human hope and searching and not to set it aside. When we say therefore that the Church is oriented towards both God and the created order we mean that as a sign of the coming kingdom it marks both the transformation and the fulfilment of human longing. *Promise* and *fulfilment* are therefore apt words to express this double orientation. Both owe their origin to the preaching of the kingdom but the one represents the sense in which the kingdom is ultimate and final, the other the sense in which it enters time and history as the definitive substance of human expectation. It is only in the fulfilment of Christ that yearning and expectation can be transformed into promise and thus assume their full and authoritative human identity.

Our analysis so far suggests that it is more appropriate to concep-
tualize the double orientation of the Church in dialectical terms. The
Church manifests the kingdom in the twin modes of promise and fulfilment but it is never possible to fix either in one particular moment
or feature of the Church's existence. To do so is to fall into the trap
of ecclesiological monophysitism. The Church is not identical with the
kingdom but it proclaims the promise of the kingdom and, in its
koinonia, already anticipates its fulfilment. Promise and fulfilment are
dialectically related in the sense that they are distinct but mutually
constitutive ways in which the kingdom reveals itself in the life of the
Church. The Church is therefore a reality oriented towards both
promise and fulfilment. It is simultaneously a sign and instrument of
the hoped-for kingdom and a foretaste and anticipation of the fulfilment of the kingdom. Its double orientation lies not in an internal
distinction between what is visible and invisible but in its constitution
by the eschatological reality of the kingdom.

V

In concluding our discussion of the ecclesiology of communion I now
want to return to the current discussion of communion within
Anglicanism. At the 1988 Lambeth conference of Anglican bishops
the terminology of 'impairment' was used to describe the situation
facing the Anglican communion following the admission of women to
the episcopate.[72] More recently the Archbishop of Canterbury's
commission on communion and women in the episcopate set up
following the Lambeth Conference and chaired by Archbishop Robin
Eames has used expressions such as 'restricted' or 'incomplete'
communion in characterizing inter-Anglican relations.[73] Confusingly
Anglicans now find themselves discussing their own internal relations
in terms that seem more appropriate to ecumenical dialogue between
separate churches.

The urgency with which the debate about the consequences of
admitting women to the episcopate and the priesthood has been
conducted is a sign of the importance of the sacred ministry in
Anglican ecclesiology. As we have already stated, Anglicanism lays
enormous stress upon the shared experience of fellowship as the basis
of its collective identity and its claim to be a communion of churches.
While Anglicans have traditionally been rather reserved about spelling
out the grounds of their communion, the mutual recognition and interchangeability of ministries has always been a part of its claim to be
more than a loose federation of national churches sharing common

historical roots. The present situation, where not all canonically ordained priests and bishops are recognized across the whole communion, represents a heightening of what many would describe as the crisis in Anglican self-identity. This is further amplified by the fact of Anglican ecclesiological minimalism. Where a Church defines its *koinonia* in terms of relatively few fundamental articles it is obviously more exposed to disruption when one or other of them is felt to be compromised.

In responding to this situation the Eames commission devoted considerable attention to the question of the pastoral care of those Anglicans who remain opposed to women priests and bishops. The commission rejected the call for parallel ecclesial jurisdictions but endorsed the proposal for episcopal visitors that first emerged in discussions within the Episcopal Church of the United States of America. Resolution B022 of the General Convention, 1988, has it that,

a. The Presiding Bishop may designate members of the House of Bishops to act as Episcopal Visitors to provide episcopal sacramental acts for congregations of this Church upon the request and under the authority and direction of the Ecclesiastical Authority of a Diocese. Nothing in this provision shall be construed as abrogating the jurisdiction of the Bishops, or Article II, Section 3 of the Constitution and the Canonical relationships between the Diocesan Bishop and the Congregation, together with its clergy.

b. The Diocesan Bishop shall notify the Presiding Bishop's office in writing of all requests and arrangements made in each case. The Presiding Bishop shall make a report in writing to each meeting of the House of Bishops.

c. This provision is only to be used for the transition and incorporation of women into all ordained ministries and is not otherwise applicable.

d. This provision shall remain in effect until the 71st General Convention and, unless re-affirmed, it shall expire upon its adjournment.[74]

This proposal met with considerable opposition and has never really been put into effect. As a result full provision for those opposed to women's ordination as priests and bishops tends to be limited to those American dioceses that have remained unreconciled to national Church policy. The situation in the Church of England is, however, very different. Following the decision to admit women to the priesthood the House of Bishops brought before the General Synod a measure to ensure that 'the integrity of differing beliefs and positions concerning the ordination of women to the priesthood should be mutually recognized and respected'.[75] In particular the Act established a mechanism for 'extended episcopal care' whereby clergy and parishes opposed to women priests would receive episcopal ministry from a bishop who shares their view on this matter. Although not spelt out in the Act of Synod or in the explanatory document *Bonds of Peace* that accompanied its publication in draft form, extended episcopal care is clearly intended as a positive response to those Anglicans who feel that communion with their diocesan bishop has been impaired by the ordination of women to the priesthood. The legislation is quite clear that this is an extension of existing episcopal care and oversight and not an alternative to it. However, it does mean that a parish that petitions its diocesan bishop under the terms of the act may receive episcopal ministry from a different bishop.

Although in practice there has been widespread acceptance of the arrangements set out in the Act of Synod, particularly the provision for provincial episcopal visitors – the so-called 'flying bishops' – reservations have been expressed about them by those on both sides of the debate about women's ordination to the priesthood. Proponents of women's ordination have suggested that extended episcopal care is inconsistent with the traditional role of the diocesan bishop in Anglican ecclesiology. Opponents have taken the same point and used it to argue that the provisions are inadequate because they do not permit parishes to move unambiguously into a new episcopal jurisdiction. It is interesting to note here that the debate on this matter is driven by a common discernment of the centrality of the episcopal office even though rather different conclusions are being drawn.

In what remains of this paper we will consider the ecclesiological implications of such a scheme and how far it can be defended, in the words of the Eames commission, 'as a necessary and strictly extraordinary anomaly in preference to schism'.[76] To Anglicans, particularly in provinces which are divided on the issue, these are matters of moment. However, in begging the forbearance of non-Anglican readers, I would point out that the discussion of extended episcopal care raises important questions that can only be answered by considering the wider issue of ecclesial *koinonia*. My hope is that in discussing this Anglican arrangement further light will be cast on the general ecclesiological issues that have already been raised.

A first point to note is that Anglicans are often guilty of centring the discussion of the Church on the theology of the ordained ministry, a tendency they are quick to criticize in others. The reasons for this are fairly clear but we do not intend to pursue them here. In our discussion of the nature of the Church we have raised questions about what might be termed its fundamental structure and identity. In short we have attempted an outline sketch of the general form of the Church as *koinonia*. What we have not done is to ask how any society of men and women exhibiting this form may lay a specific claim to be a representation of the body of Christ. It is at this point that questions of authority are raised and thus that ecclesiology necessarily takes on a specifically confessional form. At this level of discussion, where questions to do with the interpretation of the traditional 'marks' of the Church are raised, many Christians would point to the historic episcopate as a crucial element in any claim to genuine apostolicity. These are vital issues but to begin the discussion of the Church with them distorts the order of theological reflection. In his monumental study of lay ministry Yves Congar has pointed out that it has been to the impoverishment of the theology of ministry that it has customarily proceeded from hierarchology rather than ecclesiology.[77] The same criticism can be made of ecclesiology in general. Focusing the discussion of the Church almost entirely on the question of the historical expression of holy order means that the Church is understood in terms of the latter rather than *vice versa*; ecclesiology becomes, as it were, a consequence of hierarchology. Quite apart from the fact that this inverts the appropriate order of ecclesiological reflection, rendering what is consequential a matter of primary importance, this way of approaching the question distorts the genuine significance of the apostolic ministry. If the sacred ministry is a sacramental focus for the primary *koinonia* of the whole people of God then this cannot be adequately represented when the Church itself is already interpreted in the light of a narrowly defined theology of holy order. Although holy order is not simply derived from the ministry of the whole Church it exists because of it and in its service. St Cyprian understood this point, defining bishop and priest reciprocally: 'These form a Church, the people united to their high priest and the flock following its shepherd. Wherefore you must know that a bishop is constituted by his Church and a Church by its bishop'.[78] With this in mind we will examine the provisions for extended episcopal care in the light of the fundamental ecclesiology of *koinonia* rather than the specific concerns of the theology of the sacred ministry. Our argument will be that, notwithstanding difficulties at that level, the provisions can be justified as an expression of the primary identity of the Church as a *koinonia*.

We have already pointed out that people on both sides of the debate addressed by the Episcopal Ministry Act of Synod 1993 have condemned it as inconsistent with the bishop's role as principal minister in his diocese.[79] The argument is that in this matter there can be no half-measures: one is either in or out of communion with one's bishop. To intrude another episcopal figure into this relationship appears inconsistent with well-established principles of Anglican polity.[80] Against such clear-cut affirmations, and in partial defence of its suggested arrangements, the Eames commission insisted that the juridical notion of simply being 'in communion' or 'out of communion' is insufficient.[81] Apart from appealing to the evidence of growing ecumenical convergence the theological grounds of this position are not spelt out in the report, but this does not mean that they cannot be.

Earlier we described the Church as a sacramental sign of God's plan to unite all things in communion with himself. As a sacrament the Church has a double character, being orientated both to this age and the yearning for salvation and to the new age of God's kingdom. This double orientation is misrepresented if we fail to hold each in balance and lean too heavily on one or the other. Because of its eschatological character the temptation is always there to say too little or too much about the Church and thus either to absolutize or relativize it. In our discussion of this question we suggested that an appropriate balance is only achieved if we speak of the Church's orientation to the *eschaton* in terms of the dialectic of promise and fulfilment. The Church is a sacrament of God's final gift of salvation because, in its own life, it signifies that gift as both promise and fulfilment. Promise and fulfilment are dialectically related in the sense that they are the mutually constitutive modes of the kingdom's presence in and through the Church's ministry and life. The Church is promise in the sense that it points to that which it too awaits. It is fulfilment in the sense that even in declaring the promise the Church anticipates that which is promised. As an illustration of what is meant by this dialectical approach we might point to the Church's ministry of proclamation. When the Church proclaims the good news of the kingdom it clearly acts under the dialectic of promise, pointing forward to the promised fulfilment of all things. However, in declaring the promise of God the Church acts with authority because it already experiences in its own life the substance of that promise and thus corresponds also to the dialectic of fulfilment. So, for example, the writer of St John declares that when Christians speak of Christ and what he has done they do so in the power of the one who is to come, the Holy Spirit (John 14.26; 16.13). Similarly, the author of Mark's Gospel states that when Christians fulfil their ministry of proclamation it is not they who speak but the Holy Spirit (Mark 13.11), the same Spirit whose advent is the principal sign of God's kingdom come in power. The Church's spirit-filled declaration of the promise of the kingdom is also a manifestation of the power and presence of the end times.

If the Church is structured in relation to both promise and fulfilment then hope is the characteristic form of its life. Hope is precisely the hope of fulfilment but it is constituted as hope by being the eagerness and longing of those who *await* what is promised. Conversely, since there must be grounds for hope, it can only be present if there is already anticipation and foretaste. Hope is at the same time a sign of present incompleteness – one does not hope for what one already has – and a confident and faithful expectation of completion to come (Rom. 8.24-25). It is the characteristic form of life of those whose life is lived in relation to the dialectic of promise and fulfilment.

In its *koinonia* the Church is a sacramental sign of God's plan for the reconciliation of all things. It is, as various theologians have put it, the world viewed from its end. In so far as it points to the end of all things it is a sign of what is ultimate and final, but it is not itself – at least not yet – the ultimate or final community of men and women. In this context it might be more appropriate to describe the Church 'militant here on earth' as a penultimate reality, but more of that in due course. The Church's existence in relation to the *eschaton* cannot be reduced wholly to either one or other of the two modes of promise and fulfilment. As a community existing under the dialectic of promise the Church represents the world waiting 'with eager longing for the revealing of the sons of God' (Rom. 8.19). At the same time, as the community already in possession of the first fruits of the Spirit (Rom. 8.23) it exists under the dialectic of fulfilment and thus represents the world ahead of itself.

Drawing a distinction between the visible and the invisible Church and locating its 'true' character in the latter is a particular manifestation of the failure to discern the dynamic relationship of the Church to God's eschatological kingdom. As a solution to the problem of representing the double orientation of the Church to the kingdom it fails because the historical community of faith is relativized and its soteriological significance misrepresented. The eschatological priority of God's kingdom does not mean that the Church's mission is rendered impossible until it is perfected. To suggest as much is to interpret the Church entirely in terms of the dialectic of fulfilment ignoring altogether the sense in which the Church is also the community of promise. Equally questionable is the position implied by those who, in opposing the provisions of the Episcopal Ministry Act of Synod 1993, insist that one is either in or out of communion with one's bishop and that any compromise is theologically impossible. It is of course undeniable that for Anglicanism, as for catholic Christianity in general, the local expression of the Church catholic is the eucharistic community gathered around its bishop. However, to suggest that communion at this level is a matter of 'all or nothing' appears inconsistent with what we have described as the Church's double orientation to the kingdom. If the Church's relation to the kingdom is always mediated through the dialectic of promise and fulfilment then it is not possible to identify any single feature of its life as an unambiguous manifestation of either the former or the latter. But this is precisely what is implied in this case, namely, that the *koinonia* of bishop and people, unlike other manifestations of ecclesial *koinonia*, represents the Church only after the mode of fulfilment. The difficulty with any attempt to absolutize communion in one feature or moment of the Church's existence is that this in turn leads to the relativizing of other manifestations of communion. It appears that we are once again confronted with the kind of polarization that also informs the invisible/visible Church divide. Absolutizing one or other aspect of the Church's life and treating it as a signal manifestation of the Church's orientation to the fulfilment of the age to come misrepresents its double character. The *koinonia* of bishop and people is undoubtedly a key element in catholic ecclesiology but its significance is fatally misrepresented if it is treated as an exception to the Church's constitution after the dialectic of fulfilment *and* promise. It too is both a sign and an anticipation of the coming kingdom of reconciliation and peace.

So far we have approached the question of the provisions of the Act of Synod negatively, by challenging the absolutized view of episcopal *koinonia* held by some who oppose the measure. Is it possible to pass a positive judgement on its proposals for the establishment of extended episcopal care? I want to begin by quoting from a key passage in the Introduction to the Eames report. In commending the report to the Anglican communion the commission appeals for a spirit of 'respect' and 'courtesy':

When differences of principle and practice result in tension, debate and pain, such a spirit will create a profound unity and communion beyond that which the world knows. If those who find the exclusion of women from the priesthood and episcopate contrary to an understanding of God's justice and the meaning of the Incarnation, and those who find their inclusion an unacceptable development of the apostolic ministry can come together to share each other's burdens and sufferings, then the Anglican Communion will have learned something of the meaning of communion with the God who suffers. And we shall have something to say about the unity of Christians and the unity of all humankind.[82]

This invitation to seek a communion which encompasses differences in principle and practice no doubt will be dismissed by some as an example of Anglican woolly-mindedness, making a virtue out of an unfortunate necessity. However, such an appeal cannot be so lightly dismissed. As we have suggested, the ministry of the Church is not rendered impossible until it is perfected. On the contrary, it is in its very incompleteness and in an accompanying awareness of dependence upon God's promise of fulfilment that the Church bears witness to his love and mercy. St Paul understood this well, recognizing that his weakness was a sign of the efficacy of God's grace (cf. 2 Cor. 12.9; 4.7-12). There is an important sense in which 'what is lacking' in the life of the Church also serves the mission of God. One is not suggesting that sin and disorder in the Church should increase in order that grace might abound but rather that the desire to avoid schism and to embrace differences within the context of a discipleship of *koinonia* is consistent with the Church's witness to the primary sufficiency of grace. The Church's potency as a sacramental sign depends entirely upon the power of God's love. It is only when we are weak and recognise our incompleteness that we know our need of God and hence bear witness to the gratuitous nature of salvation. To say otherwise is dangerously near to suggesting that the Church ceases to be the Church when it manifests incompleteness.[83] The Church is always both promise and fulfilment. In this sense its very incompleteness, in signifying 'what is lacking', serves the mystery of God's will, pointing beyond itself to the fulfilment that it too hopes and yearns for.

The desire to embrace divisions within a wider vision of communion has led some ecumenists to describe the various historic Christian churches as 'provisional'.[84] This is an unfortunate term, suggesting as it does that the Church in this age is not already an anticipation of the fulfilment of the age to come. If the Church is merely provisional then it is difficult to see how it can be regarded as a community that already owes its existence in the present entirely to the future. It is of course true that the Church is also orientated towards this age and the yearning of men and women for fulfilment but we have been careful to insist that in this too it is constituted by the *eschaton*. It is only in the new relationships inaugurated by Christ that human yearning is transformed into hope, constituting the Church as the community of promise. We have described promise and fulfilment dialectically because both are simultaneous manifestations of the Church's constitution by the advent of God's kingdom of peace and reconciliation. As the world ahead of itself the Church exists entirely from the ultimate and definitive future.

We have been careful to insist that no single feature of the Church's life can be identified unambiguously with either the dialectic of promise or that of fulfilment. However, it is clear that the Church is not yet the ultimate community of the kingdom. Nonetheless it is entirely defined by its relationship to that kingdom. Indeed we have even spoken of 'what is lacking' in its life as also at the service of the kingdom. Paradoxically the Church signifies both the gift of salvation and the need for salvation. The Church already anticipates the fulfilment to come but awaits its final consummation. Rather than describing the historic churches as provisional it is more appropriate to speak of the Church as a penultimate human community. The Church is penultimate in the sense that, even in its incompleteness, the Christian community is defined by its relationship to the ultimate. It is only in awareness of the ultimate that human life can be transformed into a discipleship of hope and thus become a *diakonia*[85] of the kingdom. Describing the Church as provisional exaggerates its contingency, ignoring the sense in which its life already represents the transformation of human yearning into the hope and promise of the ultimate. The Church is a penultimate community in the sense that it exists entirely at the service of the ultimate. It is a community of men and women struggling to realise in their own lives the obedience of faith which is the *koinonia* of the Holy Spirit. In this light it is possible to offer a favourable judgement on the Anglican communion's struggle to maintain unity in the face of internal divisions over doctrine and practice. Is it not possible to see in, for example, the provision of extended episcopal care a genuine act of *koinonia* discipleship on the part of Anglicans? From the point of view of the theology of ministry this appears anomalous, a compromise designed as a concession to circumstances, but seen against the wider background of an ecclesiology of *koinonia* it is possible to view it more positively as representing a recognition of the penultimacy of the Church. It is in a small way an action in the service of the ultimate state of humanity – 'that they all may be one'.

Notes

1. Perry Butler, 'From the Early Eighteenth Century to the Present Day' in S.W. Sykes and J. Booty, ed., *The Study of Anglicanism* (SPCK, London, 1988), p. 29.
2. See, for example, resolutions 48 and 49 of the Lambeth Conference of 1930 where it is stated that 'The Anglican Communion is a fellowship ...

bound together not by a central legislative and executive authority but by mutual loyalty, sustained by the common counsel of the bishops in conference'. R. Coleman, *Resolutions of the Twelve Lambeth Conferences 1867-1988* (Anglican Book Centre, Toronto, 1992), pp. 83ff.

3. The First Report, 60. Reprinted in *The Eames Commission: The Official Reports. The Archbishop of Canterbury's Commission on Communion and Women in the Episcopate* (Anglican Book Centre, Toronto, 1994).

4. J. Robert Wright, ed., *A Communion of Communions: One Eucharistic Fellowship* (Seabury Press, New York, 1979), pp. 231-2.

5. Quoted in P. Avis, *Anglicanism and the Christian Church* (T & T Clark, Edinburgh, 1989), p. 305.

6. ibid., p. 306.

7. For a more detailed discussion of this use of the idea of family resemblance see R. Hannaford, 'Anglican Family Resemblance' in Michael Watts, ed., *Through a Glass Darkly: A Crisis Considered* (Gracewing Fowler Wright Books, Leominster, 1993), pp. 53-74, and R. Hannaford, 'Anglican Identity and Ecumenism' in *Journal of Ecumenical Studies* 32:2 (Spring 1995), pp. 195-206.

8. See Michael Kinnamon, ed., *Signs of the Spirit* (WCC Publications & Eerdmans, Geneva & Grand Rapids, 1991), pp. 172-174.

9. See Thomas F. Best & Gunther Gassman, ed., *On the Way to Fuller Koinonia: Official Report of the Fifth World Conference on Faith and Order. Faith and Order Paper No. 166* (WCC Publications, Geneva, 1994).

10. *Fifth Forum on Bilateral Conversations. Faith and Order Paper No. 156* (WCC Publications, Geneva, 1989), p. 46.

11. *Ways to Community* (Lutheran World Federation, Geneva, 1980).

12. *Church as Communion: An Agreed Statement by the Second Anglican-Roman Catholic International Commission* (Church House Publishing & Catholic Truth Society, London, 1991).

13. *Christifideles laici* 18, Apostolic Exhortation on the Laity.

14. J.M.R.Tillard, *Church of Churches: The Ecclesiology of Communion* (The Liturgical Press, Collegeville Minnesota, 1992).

15. Jerome Hamer OP., *The Church is a Communion* (Geoffrey Chapman, London, 1964).

16. Tillard, op.cit., p. xi.

17. Robert Kress, *The Church: Communion, Sacrament, Communication* (Paulist Press, New York, 1985).

18. George H. Tavard, *The Church, Community of Salvation* (The Liturgical Press, Collegeville Minnesota, 1992).

19. Paul Avis, *Christians in Communion* (Geoffrey Chapman Mowbray, London, 1990).

20. John Reuman, '*Koinonia* in Scripture: Survey of Biblical Texts' in Thomas F. Best & Gunther Gassmann, ed., *On the Way to Fuller Koinonia: Official Report of the Fifth World Conference on Faith and Order. Faith and Order Paper No. 166* (WCC Publications, Geneva, 1994), pp. 37-69.

21. *The Final Report by the First Anglican-Roman Catholic International Commission* (Catholic Truth Society/SPCK,London, 1982), p. 5f.

22. cf. *Church as Communion: An Agreed Statement by the Second Anglican-Roman Catholic International Commission*, 3.

23. Karl Barth, *Church Dogmatics* I/1 (ET. G.T. Thompson, T & T Clark, Edinburgh, 1936); Karl Rahner, *The Trinity* (Burns and Oates, Tunbridge Wells, 1970).

24. See, for example, Jürgen Moltmann's trenchant criticism of Barth and Rahner in *The Trinity and the Kingdom of God* (SCM, London, 1981), pp. 154-161.

25. In point of fact, although he rejects all social analogies of the trinity, Barth does envisage a communion within God himself. However, unlike Moltmann who conceives this in terms of personal relationships *within* the godhead, Barth approaches this as an aspect of the single divine personhood of God by treating the Holy Spirit as the communion of the Father and the Son. The Holy Spirit's mode of existence is the mutual 'participation of the Father and the Son ... the *common factor* between the mode of existence of God the Father and that of God the Son' (*Church Dogmatics* III/1, p. 537). Barth's approach is not without its difficulties. In particular it is not clear how the transition is made from the 'commonness' in the origin of the Spirit (i.e. in relation to the Father and the Son) to the concept of community. Barth begins to address this when he asserts that knowledge of the divine communion revealed in the Holy Spirit is knowledge of the ground of communion in the eternal community of Father and Son (*Church Dogmatics* III/1, p. 549f., and II/1, p. 63f., 307f, 313). In other words God's communion with humanity is possible only because God is eternally present to himself as the communion of the Father and the Son. The Spirit is God revealed as communion, love and gift and as such is the source and ground of our human knowledge of the trinity. For a significant re-working of Barth's thinking on this point see Claude Welch, *The Trinity in Contemporary Theology* (SCM, London, 1953), pp. 200-203, 281-290.

26. Moltmann, op.cit., p. 157.

27. ibid.

28. J.R. Illingworth, *The Doctrine of the Trinity* (Macmillan and Co., London, 1907), p. 143f.

29. L.S. Thornton, *The Incarnate Lord* (Longmans, Green and Co. Ltd, London, 1928), p. 411.

30. ibid., p. 415f.

31. ibid., p. 305.

32. ibid., p. 356.

33. ibid., p. 304.

34. ibid., p. 416. This line of thought is also developed in Thornton's contribution to *Essays Catholic and Critical*, ed., Selwyn, 'The Christian Conception of God', p. 139ff.

35. Leonardo Boff, *Trinity and Society* (Burns and Oates, Tunbridge Wells, 1988), p. 136.

36. *The Forgotten Trinity* 1, The Report of the British Council of Churches Study Commission on Trinitarian Doctrine Today (British Council of Churches, London, 1989), para. 7.3.
37. Colin E. Gunton, *The One, The Three and the Many: God, Creation and the Culture of Modernity* (CUP, Cambridge, 1993).
38. ibid., p. 214.
39. See J.D. Zizioulas, *Being as Communion: Studies in Personhood and the Church* (Darton, Longman and Todd, London, 1985).
40. Gunton, op.cit., p. 217. While Gunton notes that Christology and Pneumatology are essential to an understanding of communion he does not explain how this can be transposed into the discussion of ecclesiology.
41. ibid., p. 222.
42. Gunton acknowledges his debt to Daniel Hardy's work on sociality. See Hardy's 'Created and Redeemed Sociality' in C.E. Gunton and D.W. Hardy, ed., *On Being the Church. Essays on the Christian Community* (T & T Clark, Edinburgh, 1989), pp. 21-47.
43. Gunton, op.cit., p. 167.
44. R. D. Williams, 'Trinity and Ontology' in K. Surin, ed., *Christ, Ethics and Tragedy: Essays in Honour of Donald MacKinnon* (CUP, Cambridge, 1989), p. 78.
45. In an unpublished paper, 'Is a "trinitarian ontology" possible?', forthcoming in *Modern Theology*.
46. Rahner, op.cit., p. 21ff.
47. D.M. MacKinnon 'The Relation of the Doctrines of the Incarnation and the Trinity' in Richard W. A. McKinney, ed., *Creation, Christ and Culture, Studies in Honour of T.F. Torrance* (T & T Clark, Edinburgh, 1976), p. 104.
48. R.D. Williams, op.cit., p. 84.
49. W. Kasper, *The God of Jesus Christ* (SCM, London, 1983), p. 248. Karl Barth, *Church Dogmatics* II/2 (T & T Clark, Edinburgh, 1957), p. 3, makes much the same point in his famous statement that 'Originally God's election of man is a predestination not merely of man but of himself'. For Barth the Christian doctrine of God has its foundation in the formal structure of revelation and not simply in its content. Hence he insists that the Father's objectivity to himself in the Son and the Holy Spirit is a condition of his secondary objectivity in revelation.
50. A point made very effectively by Archimandrite Vasileios, *Hymn of Entry: Liturgy and Life in the Orthodox Church* (ET Elizabeth Brière, St Vladimir's Seminary Press, Crestwood/New York, 1984), p. 17f: 'This new family – the body of Christ and the communion of the Holy Spirit – is responsible for writing the Gospel, which is not a systematic exposition of Christian teaching, precisely because it is not concerned with teaching. Jesus did not leave behind Him a new philosophical system, nor did He institute a mere religion. He left His body and sent His Spirit. And the Gospel consists of fundamental elements from the life of Jesus and the experience of the new community in Christ ... those things

which the world could not contain if they were written in detail are found, made known and lived in the Church, where Jesus Himself lives'.

51. J. Zizioulas, op.cit., p. 19.

52. Gunton, op.cit., p. 217.

53. John Robinson, *The Body* (SCM, London, 1952), p. 47.

54. Other relevant New Testament passages, apart from the Johannine references, include, Col. 1.15-17; Heb. 1.2-3; Rev. 1.17.

55. See W. Kasper, *Jesus the Christ* (Burns and Oates, London, 1976), pp. 185-192; Hans Küng, *Justification. The Doctrine of Karl Barth and a Catholic Reflection* (Burns and Oates, London, re-issued 1981), pp. 125ff, 135ff, 285ff; W. Pannenberg, *Jesus God and Man* (SCM, London, 1968), pp. 168f; H. Riedlinger, 'How Universal is Christ's Kingship?', pp. 56-65 & O. Rousseau, 'The Idea of the Kingship of Christ', pp. 67-74, both in *Concilium*, January 1966.

56. W. Kasper, *Jesus the Christ*, p. 185.

57. Quoted in A.M. Allchin, 'The True Substance of Joy', *Theology* vol. LXII no 465, March 1959, p. 107.

58. Colin E. Gunton, op.cit., p. 215.

59. A.T. & R.P.C. Hanson, *The Identity of the Church: A Guide to Recognizing the Contemporary Church* (SCM, London, 1987), p. ix.

60. The claim that *koinonia* belongs not just to the being of the Church but also to its calling in the way of the cross is only sketched in outline here. A more detailed consideration of the question would invite parallels with Christology. How are we to understand Christ's *koinonia* with the Father? If we stress Christ's ontological unity with the Father are we not in danger of denying that his human life marks the fulfilment of creaturely obedience to and union with the Godhead? As *the* fundamental sacrament of divine/human *koinonia* Christ's union with the Father must be understood as to do with both the eternal gift of life and being from the Father and the faithful obedience of Jesus. Jesus is not only one with the Father in terms of being; he also learnt obedience through suffering. We must speak of his *koinonia* with the Father as a matter of will as well as of nature. It does not do to speak of Christ's communion with the Father as either ontological or existential; it is both.

61. The sacramental model of the Church is gaining ground in catholic ecclesiology. See, for example, Henri de Lubac, *Catholicism. Christ and the Common Destiny of Man* (Burns and Oates, London, 1950), p. 28, who is usually credited with having revived this way of understanding the Church; Avery Dulles, *Models of the Church* (Gill and Macmillan, Dublin, 1976), pp. 58-70; Walter Kasper, *Theology and Church* (SCM, London, 1989), pp. 111-128; Karl Rahner, *The Church and the Sacraments* (Burns and Oates, London, 1974), pp. 11-75, 'Membership of the Church According to the Teaching of Pius XII's Encyclical *Mystici Corporis Christi*' in *Theological Investigations* (Darton, Longman & Todd, London, 1963), vol. 2, pp. 1-88, *Foundations of Christian Faith* (Darton, Longman & Todd, London/Seabury, New York, 1978), pp. 411-13; Karl Ratzinger, *Principles of Catholic Theology. Building Stones for*

a Fundamental Theology (Ignatius Press, San Francisco, 1987), pp. 44-54; E. Schillebeeckx, *Christ The Sacrament of Encounter with God* (Sheed & Ward, London, 1963). While the sacramental model has not received much attention outside catholic ecclesiology there is a discussion of it by the Protestant theologian Eberhard Jüngel. See his 'The Church as Sacrament?' in *Eberhard Jüngel: Theological Essays* (T & T Clark, Edinburgh, 1989), pp. 189-213. It was also adopted by the Anglican theologian H. Burn-Murdock in *Church, Continuity and Unity* (CUP, Cambridge, 1945), pp. 31-37.

62. *Church as Communion: An Agreed Statement by the Second Anglican-Roman Catholic International Commission*, 17.

63. Karl Rahner, *The Church and the Sacraments*, pp. 11-19.

64. Karl Rahner, *Foundations of Christian Faith*, pp. 411-413.

65. Henri de Lubac, *Catholicism. Christ and the Common Destiny of Man*, p. 29.

66. Vatican II, *Dogmatic Constitution on the Church [Lumen Gentium]*, 1, 9, & 48.

67. *Ut Unum Sint. Encyclical Letter of the Holy Father John Paul II On Commitment to Ecumenism*, 5 (Catholic Truth Society, London, 1995).

68. For a more extensive discussion of this see Robert Hannaford, 'Foundations for an Ecclesiology of Ministry' in C. Hall & R. Hannaford, ed., *Order and Ministry* (Gracewing Fowler Wright, Leominster, 1996), pp. 21-60.

69. Edward Schillebeeckx, op. cit., p. 55f.

70. J.D. Zizioulas, op. cit., p. 233.

71. ibid., p. 185f.

72. See, for example, the sectional report on 'Mission and Ministry', 150 in *The Truth Shall Make You Free: The Lambeth Conference 1988* (Church House Publishing, London, 1988), p. 61.

73. The First Report, 150, *The Eames Commission: The Official Reports*, p. 31.

74. Quoted in *The Eames Commission: The Official Reports*, p. 29f.

75. *Episcopal Ministry Act of Synod 1993*.

76. The First Report, 55, *The Eames Commission: The Official Reports*, p. 30.

77. Yves M. J. Congar, *Lay People in the Church. A Study for a Theology of Laity* (Geoffrey Chapman, London, 1959), pp. 22-52.

78. Cyprian, *Ep*. lxvi. 8.

79. cf. Canon C18, Church of England Canons.

80. See, for example, *Episcopal Ministry: The Report of the Archbishops' Group on the Episcopate 1990* (Church House Publishing, London, 1990).

81. The First Report, 56. See *The Eames Commission: The Official Reports*, p. 31.

82. Introduction, 12. See *The Eames Commission: The Official Reports*, p. 13.

83. This is another reason for feeling uneasy about Zizioulas' rhythmic

understanding of the Church's relation to the *eschaton*. Are we to understand that the Church ceases to exist as the Church during the intervals between eucharistic celebrations?

84. See, for example, Christian Duquoc, *Provisional Churches* (SCM, London, 1986).

85. *Diakonia* is usually translated as 'ministry' or 'service' but see the important new study of this New Testament word and its cognates in John N. Collins, *Diakonia: Re-interpreting the Ancient Sources* (OUP, Oxford/New York, 1990).

The Christological Centre of Anglicanism

Tim Bradshaw

Introduction – Some Reflections on Where We Are

What are the central problems for Anglicanism as it looks into the future? In a sense the tragic final *Crockford's Preface*[1] set out the fears of the conservative churchman with great clarity. Anglicanism faces the choice of going liberal in a radical sense, or staying with the inherited tradition, a conservative and dogmatic church, reformed catholicism. That preface predicted that the ordination of women would mean a break with that tradition. But the *Preface* asked other probing questions about the bonds which unite Anglicans, now that the common factor of the Book of Common Prayer is no longer in place and the claim that a single liturgy unites no longer applies. Worldwide, Anglicanism is a diverse communion, ranging from the ultra politically correct and unorthodox Americans, to the evangelicals of Africa and the remaining Anglo-Catholics.

The *Crockford's Preface* predicted that the radical transatlantic influence would prove too great to be resisted, and would drag other parts of the church into its slipstream. Whether this will happen is not at all certain. The ordination of women was argued on scriptural grounds, not simply by way of cutting free from the authority of scripture, and thus far the Church of England has not shown signs that this change has meant the destruction of the old authority pattern of Scripture and tradition in favour of baptising the mores of ultra-modern freedom. In England, which is my main focus, Anglicanism still has a conservative drag, not only from within its own parish membership and leadership, but also from public opinion and especially the media, which likes to keep its church as it found it before it stopped attending it. An interesting instance of this is the outcry over modern forms of inclusive language in the popular press.

It may be that the confidence of liberal theology is now eroding fast

90

as the Western liberal project for humanity, rooted in the Enlightenment, is increasingly perceived to have failed. Some social analysts, formerly in the vanguard of the confident secular liberal ethos dictating social policy since 1945 in the United Kingdom, seem to be having second thoughts as the moral consensus collapses. This finds echoes in the theological world. Tom Oden's book, *Agenda for Theology: After Modernity What?*[2] provides a powerful analysis of the way an ordinary modernist theologian, who had been taking the high road of liberal scholarship and thought, deeply influenced by the existentialist philosophers and pyschologists, suddenly found himself at the edge, looking into the abyss, at the end of that road. According to Oden, now a repentant Bultmannian, a wilful adolescent attitude now characterises Western culture. In philosophical terms this amounts to a Nietzschean cutting-free from tradition and a reconstruction of society and the self. 'In sum', he says, 'nothing is more characteristic of postmodern consciousness than the unwillingness to be parented by historical reason and the wisdom of social experience'.[3] He lists the axial assumptions of modern Western culture, in what he regards as its state of disintegration, as: 'contempt for premodern wisdoms, absolutized moral relativism, the adolescent refusal of parenting, idealization of autonomous individualism, awed deference to reductionistic naturalism'.[4]

Oden sees modernity unravelling the skein of civilised behaviour in the troubled alliance between an optimistic evolutionary progressivism and regressive forms of nativist narcissistic hedonism. This American theologian has doubled back to the roots of Christian tradition and now nourishes himself on biblical and patristic theology and spirituality as resources for the pastoral ministry. The *Crockford's Preface* was signalling precisely such concerns in its warning to the Lambeth Conference, and the traditionalist warning is clearly becoming less unfashionable as social and cultural developments call liberal optimism into question.

The context is now no longer that of an intellectually triumphant radicalism and an intellectually terrified conservatism: both sides face powerful sets of questions and hopefully will become humbler dialogue partners, less mutually contemptuous, in future. There are signs that the advocates of radical theology in the Church of England have been shown that there are some limits to freedom of theological expression. The Bishop of Chichester, for example, drew the line at a presbyter teaching that the term 'God' refers not to an objective reality but a way of talking.[5] The Bishops' report *Issues in Human Sexuality*[6] reaffirmed the biblical and patristic basis for ethics and marriage as the normative pattern for sexual relationships, rejecting the call for ordination of practising homosexuals. The radical juggernaut may be slowing, although large numbers of Anglo-Catholics and Evangelicals remain to be convinced, and are particularly worried at the prospect of the next Lambeth Conference. Church assemblies and synods have become almost synonymous with a dynamic for change.

The relationship between the Church of England and society, and in particular the process of mutual influence, grows in significance as a factor in the church's self-understanding. General Synod declined even to set up a working party on the issue of some kind of mutation of establishment, and the idea that the church's ethical stance must shadow that of society if she is to retain 'a voice' has wide currency. The Church of England has been far from being a compliant poodle for recent governments, but her pronouncements are predictably socio-economic in tone. The danger for any established church is being too cosy and conformed to the image of the current social mores, rather than striving for the mind of Christ.

To put this in strictly theological terms, as did the 1934 Barmen Declaration, the national church could conceivably unchurch herself by becoming a purely cultural national religion, the ethical and spiritual glue of society, of a syncretistic type. Some regard this as happening incipiently in such events as the Westminster Abbey Commonwealth Service, where all faiths chime in under the roof of Anglicanism. Establishment, while having some important virtues, lends itself to state religion; the concern is that the Church of England, and indeed the Anglican Communion, do not lose hold of that which makes them a church of Jesus Christ. Some hostile critics of the Church of England think this is happening. Cardinal Newman, in his *Apologia Pro Vita Sua* gave his opinion:

> Doubtless the National Church has hitherto been a serviceable breakwater against doctrinal errors, more fundamental than its own. How long this will last in the years before us, it is impossible to say, for the Nation drags down its Church to its own level.[7]

Newman felt that the best Roman Catholic attitude towards the Church of England was not to seek to undermine it for the present while it was broadly orthodox. 'What our duty would be at another time and in other circumstances, supposing for example the Establishment lost its dogmatic faith ... is quite another matter.'[8] Some commentators feel this time has indeed come. 'Whether the point has been reached at which Newman's misgivings about Anglicanism should be heeded is a moot point. Many converts from Anglicanism would say so.'[9]

The Roman Catholic author, Clifford Longley, considers that the

Church of England is divided and unsure of itself, 'its grip on Christian doctrine is slowly weakening ... The ordination of women represents the final abandonment of the dogmatic principle as the testbed for all innovations and developments'.[10] Interestingly he thinks that in a secular society the status of establishment is a major disadvantage to any denomination, the reverse opinion to that held by General Synod.

Newman's prediction that the established church would be dragged down to the level of society's spiritual values is well worth noting; he clearly feared that the mutuality of church and nation would work predominantly in one direction. It may have been a characteristically polemical point, but it is an important one. Anglican educational and social thinking can be accused, in the second half of this century, of constantly minimizing any specifically Christian contribution to the wider discussion of social policy. This is done in the name of charity to all opinions, accepting the 'cheeseboard' approach; some suspect that it will result in the church itself acting as the board, failing to present its own flavour of cheese at all.

The policy of the Church of England is to play the role of strictly neutral advisor, to bracket her own Christian identity, and to accept relativistic and pluralist presuppositions. Perhaps the status of establishment has bred a version of 'white middle-class guilt', which the Church of England would be better without, and in this sense perhaps Clifford Longley is correct in regarding establishment as an incubus in a secular society.

The church must constantly affirm her identity as centred in Christ and the Gospel, and to seek deliberately to bracket this and prefer an identity grounded in values acceptable to society, does put at risk the status of being a church. This is a temptation for the Church of England as she seeks to be 'user friendly' in a more secular climate, however that be defined.[11] The temptation to seek an identity which least offends social mores in order to retain 'relevance' seems to be strong, but it is unchristian, false to Anglicanism and must be rejected firmly.[12]

The church's advice to the nation prior to the liberalising of the divorce law in the 1969 legislation illustrates this. The church's document *Putting Asunder* (1966) affirmed that since most of the nation was not Christian, the church's advice must be based on non-theological assumptions shared by all. Oliver O'Donovan expresses the church's principles as: 'when the church contributes to public debate on matters of concern to secular society at large, it should forget that it is the church of Jesus Christ and should address society on terms common to all participants'.[13] Whether, in fact, church bureaucracy is sensitive to the ethical assumptions of society at large is highly questionable.[14]

It is now commonly accepted, even by some of the secular proponents of the change, that the liberalised legislation proved baneful to family stability. Since the Church of England lent her support to that legislation, she must accept some of the blame and examine herself accordingly. In particular she needs to ask whether she accommodated her distinctively Christian message to the secular voices of the day. To put the matter in New Testament terms, has she been a blind guide? Paradoxically, the policy of dualism, forgetting christological loyalty in addressing the nation, proves to make the church less relevant to debates on social policy: why should a 'secular' society listen to an echo of itself? A vigorous Christian voice would be of far more interest, as well as being truly of the church.

1. Christological Centre of the Church

Anglican pastoral practice enacts a theology of concentric circles, at the centre of which is the holy trinity, the object of our worship and the source of our redemption. We believe that God is working in many ways and at different levels in people's lives and in social structures. But we are committed as a church to focus our faith on God revealed and mediated in and through Jesus. That is our central vision, and from that vision we read society and the work of God generally. God can reveal himself through a blossoming shrub, a summer's day, a Mozart concerto or a dead dog, as Barth says, and we do well to listen if he does;[15] but the Church is founded on the unique act of God in Christ.

Anglican practice accepts the many circles and types of commitment and faith; it is inclusive to an indecent degree. Quench not the smoking flax. Anglican theologians such as Coleridge and Maurice were seeking to make positive theological connections between the world and the Church long before Vatican II recognised the divine hand at work in secular society. It is very hard to be cast out of an Anglican congregation. People belong at very different stages, but the Church aims to bring them to the centre, to the feet of Christ. Our doctrine or practice of charitable presumption, the refusal to judge the spiritual state of people who want somehow to belong, shows both the commitment to the concentric circles and the insistence that this solar system has its centre of gravity.[16]

This christological, or trinitarian, centre-circumference analogy perhaps exemplifies the ongoing attraction of neo-platonic thought for

Anglican theology. F.D. Maurice, taken up by Michael Ramsey, reinstated this tradition of logos theology, the Johannine message that the light that lightens every man was coming into the world. But Ramsey did not collapse Christology into logos theology, always retaining the concreteness of Jesus Christ as well as the universal work of God through him.[17] Ontologically, for sure, there is a central Christology, while we also know that the Word works secretly in many and various ways in the world.

2. The Covenant Community of Christ

Romans 9–11 speaks of God's covenant with his people and the difficulties of its inclusiveness and exclusiveness. The Gentiles are now to be grafted onto the olive tree of faith through Jesus Christ, by the grace of God. This is a trinitarian reality, 'God has sent the Spirit of his Son into our hearts, whereby we cry Abba, Father' (Gal. 4.6). We find ourselves in fellowship with the Father through the Son, in the power of the Spirit. By the grace of God we have been bonded into communion, *koinonia*, fellowship with the life of God.

'It is the God who said "let light shine out of darkness" who has shone into our hearts, to give the light of the knowledge of the glory of God in the face of Christ' (2 Cor. 4.6). The love and generosity of the creator God, an important point of emphasis for Anglican theology, has reached out redemptively. This God evokes our response by the Spirit, and evokes our good works.[18] Such is the depth of the bond of communion constituting the Church, made possible by the death and resurrection of Jesus, and the outpouring of the Spirit. 'This communion is participation in the life of God through Christ in the Holy Spirit, making Christians one with each other.'[19] The Church is this communion, christological and trinitarian; her structures and patterns of life must be formed and measured in this light.

The covenant people of God are in communion with Christ; they are not Christ. The Church is fallible in every sense. She needs to repent, to bring herself under the scrutiny of the gospel and to reform herself accordingly. Peter's acknowledgement of the rightness of incorporating believing Gentiles into the Church, when faced with Paul's exposition of the gospel's implications, is a classic example of this happening. The sheer fact of Jesus Christ's cross and resurrection, taken with the giving of the Spirit, cracked open Petrine exclusiveness. Jesus is the second Adam, opening a new way for all humanity.

The christological gospel focus defines the Church in many dimensions. The understanding of the Church set out in the Thirty-Nine

Articles of Religion speaks of the congregation of the faithful in which the word is preached and the sacraments celebrated. Both word and sacraments nurture the congregation. The Church needs the ministry of the word and sacrament to foster the apostolic faith and life of the priestly people of God. She stands under the word in self-scrutiny, *semper reformanda*. This is distinctively Anglican, refusing to deify the Church while holding the visible Church and its historic structures in high regard as belonging to the *bene esse* of the Church.

The Church has the character of reformed catholicism because of her adherence to the way, the truth and the life, in worship, ethics and doctrine. Fellowship with the apostolic message and testimony of Christ brings catholicity; the insistence on giving this apostolicity a normative place in the Church is the commitment to the principle of *semper reformanda* of the Reformation. The Reformation did not give birth to a new church in England, but cut away accretions and revalidated the church as apostolic.

The church continues in covenant with the Apostles and Prophets in the fact that the faith has been lived and handed on from the Apostles and their converts; the first disciples were the Apostles, who were therefore the Church in the first place, although they also continued the faith of Israel. The Apostles also provided the initial forms of ministry in the Church; the ministries of the Church therefore also relate back to their ministry, presbyteral, diaconal, missiological and theological.

The unique role of the Apostles' witness to Christ, as preservers of the teaching and of the very impression created by Jesus, cannot be repeated. In that sense the Apostles are foundations on which the succeeding disciples and Church leaders stand as the house. The apostolic and prophetic witness and teaching remains with the Church through Scripture, a living symphony of their voices. The succeeding Church is in covenant with this symphony. Catholicity means living out this music of the gospel in the Spirit today. The ministry serves this purpose, not creating apostolicity but serving it.

The Church has often sought to bury the word, as the religious leaders of Jerusalem sought to bury Jeremiah who brought the word of judgement to his people, in great agony, while remaining totally committed to them and part of them. The word he brought was not a product of the people's religiosity, but he himself was one of the community to which the word came, echoing the coming of the incarnate word, 'to his own', who received him not. Communion with the word, with Christ, is covenant with the one who loves so passionately as to judge and sanctify. The Church to be truly 'Petrine' will characteristically be the repenting community, and repentance will include, *a fortiori*, that of the religious leadership.

The church is not *sufficiently* defined by the Thirty-Nine Articles. She is indeed the congregation of the faithful with sacraments and the word, but she is also the body of Christ. While even Roman Catholic exegetes now interpret this phrase as metaphorical,[20] it is metaphorical for a reality akin to the metaphor. The Church described as the body of Christ is an organic unity working with mutual self-giving as the inner dynamic. This deeply apostolic understanding of the Church rules out mechanistic and juridical models of her being.

The body excludes pride and exclusivism, hence the deep link between the description of the Church as the body and the eucharistic sharing of the one loaf, the one cup, the sacrifice of Christ in sacramental form. Christ informs the mode of being of the Church, and especially the self-sacrificing Christ; we have been baptised into the death of the Lord. This is a matter of the visible, tangible church: paradoxically to seek to reserve it for some spiritual, invisible realm would be to avoid the cross: such a mode of life is costly Christian discipleship in practice, not in idea.

The Church of England's inclusive polity implies a 'centre-circumference' view of the Church, applied in several dimensions. Christ centres the Church, and the ministry of the people of God is to worship and bring others to worship. The parish system has this sharp focus, seeking to draw all to the foot of the cross. There are many forms of contact with the visible church, and the aim of all these forms is christocentric, going out so as to bring in to the heart of faith. The future of Anglicanism, especially of the Church of England, depends heavily upon this pattern of pastoral activity being informed with the evangelistic desire to draw all to Christ. The negation of this would be for the church to drift centrifugally from her centre, to sever connection from her head, and to replace that with sociological analysis.

Another way in which the centre-circumference model[21] works in the polity of the Church of England is the distinction between the church visible and invisible. 'For lack of diligent observing the difference, first between the Church of God mystical and visible, then between the visible sound and corrupted, sometimes more sometimes less, the oversights are neither few nor light that have been committed', is the opinion of Richard Hooker.[22] The church visible is a group of people of all kinds at many stages of life and purity. The Church of England exercises 'charitable presumption' in dealing with people, assuming they mean what they say, and being anxious not to exclude, in the hope that even the unlikeliest disciples will move closer to Christ. Furthermore, ultimately only God knows the heart, and the church must leave the judgement to God. In terms of infant baptism, for example, a parent's desire to have a baby baptised and willingness to make the baptismal promises cannot finally be denied.

The parish structure covering the whole nation includes everyone, rejecting none and calling all to faith in Christ. This christocentrism works in and through the ethic of serving the local community, rather than being an alternative to it. Transformation and new possibilities come from faith and this informs the zeal for serving others which theoretically suffuses the parish congregation. Anglicanism is not primarily about fitting in with the current social mores, bracketing her loyalty to Jesus Christ in order to retain social acceptability. Rather the church seeks to forward faith and worship in its care for the community.

3. The Irenaean Shape of the Church

The Anglican tradition of simple, reformed catholicism, 'mere Christianity', rests on a biblical theology but also the patristic tradition of faith and ethics. Irenaeus, Bishop of Lyons *c.*177, whose heritage came from the eastern church, may illustrate the distinctive emphases of the Anglican tradition. He ministered in a context of gnosticism and syncretism, of many competing spiritualities and religions. His theological response was to affirm the unity of God as creator and redeemer. This was in the face of the challenge of Marcion who questioned the goodness of the Old Testament creator God in contrast to the loving God of the New Testament.

Irenaeus appealed to the Scriptures, both Old and New Testaments, maintaining the Hebraic tradition of God as the background matrix of interpretation for the person of Jesus. An alternative might have been to plug Jesus into a gnostic context of thought, leading to some very different doctrinal and ethical consequences. Irenaeus strongly affirms the four Gospels over against gnostic gospels, marking out the four as canonical for the Church. He produced a short 'rule of faith' or summary of the Christian credal understanding of God, Christ, the Spirit, the Church and the final coming judgement. The incarnation of the word relates closely to the restoration of creation in his theology. Christ is the second Adam who re-runs the course of the wayward first Adam, bringing humanity back to its true destiny. The human physical state of the incarnate word brings back the image to that originally created and intended by God. The physical aspect of Jesus is affirmed with great emphasis as vital for salvation. Irenaeus resists Platonic dualism of spirit versus matter: he is thoroughly Hebraic in emphasising the full humanity of Jesus for the renewal of creation and communion with God.

We can see that these emphases equate well with those of classical

Anglicanism, the commitment to the wholeness of Scripture (although we remember that the canon had not been finally formalised in his day), the closeness of the link between creation and incarnation, the simple rule of faith and affirmation of the world in all aspects, resisting dualism. Also his view of the fall, that Adam failed to realise the potential given by God, has been claimed by leading Anglican thinkers, such as Michael Ramsey,[23] dissatisfied with the radical Augustinian view which seems to verge into Manichaeism in its understanding of original sin.

The doctrine of the Church relates to the new humanity restored in the second Adam who fulfilled the will of the Father for creation. The Church is apostolic in preaching the same catholic faith openly and publicly. The bishop is the trustee of the gospel, primarily a reliable teaching figure in the line of teachers and stewards of the catholic faith, its doctrinal content and its universality, held in distinction to the gnostics.

Apostolic succession, for Irenaeus, concerns succession in true apostolic doctrine handed on by reliable teachers in the churches, the bishops. He claimed to have been taught by Polycarp, who was taught by the Apostle John in Asia. Apostolic succession was not linked with the transfer of grace at this time. Rome is taken by Irenaeus as a major church representative of the faith of all.[24] Rome did not dictate, however, to other churches, as is shown by the fact that Ireneaus stood by his own traditional dating of Easter against the Roman one. Churches were in agreement on the faith, but no one church dominated others.

Anglicans follow Irenaeus of Lyons in valuing bishops as reliable teaching figures in the Church, 'shepherds, watchmen, stewards' in the phrase of the Book of Common Prayer. Likewise he insisted on the simple yet profound catholic faith shared by churches far and wide, he respected Rome as a sister church, but equally he respected his own ancient custom and usage as just as valid and valuable.

The anti-spiritualising, anti-gnosticism of Irenaeus may also find an echo in Anglican concern for social justice, actual praxis, exemplified in its report *Faith in the City*[25] in England, but also world-wide by the South African Anglican part in the struggle for democracy from the earliest days. On the other hand, one might ask about the consistency of establishment with early patristic theology; does not the Church need to be wholly free from state interference to be the Church of Jesus, the new Adam? The Church of England alone in the Anglican Communion needs to face up to this question. Does the *Christus Victor* encompass a victory of cosmic dimensions, including a victory over the power of the state? This apart, the Irenaean ethos of theology and Church is peculiarly parallel with the Anglican in its affirmation of creation and dislike of neo-platonic spiritualising. It is a model worth taking up and using for the purposes of self-identity.

4. The Debate With Culture

The fact that Irenaeus had to minister in a context of many competing spiritual and religious claims, and succeeded in forming a workable theology and ecclesiology in so doing, has an important message for the Church today. He worked from the Christology which is interpreted against the background of the Hebrew God of creation. The person of Christ is defined in relation to the four Gospels in all their authentic historicity, in contrast to the gnostic gospels. The concreteness of this approach commends itself: the historical person of Jesus, the Apostles handing on their witness to Christian teachers in the Churches.

The Church of England is today a trustee of this catholic *kerygma*, this gospel. This is not a complex or subtle philosophy but testimony to the fact of Christ and the triune God who has acted in the cross, resurrection and sending of the Spirit. The Church simply needs to maintain this witness and worship; that is her primary ministry in the world. The task of the Church is not mainly to produce a philosophy which will explain the world, perhaps using her dogmatic and liturgical symbols as ways of illustrating a credible modern interpretation of how things are. Rather she is charged with building the community of those who are saved from the sin of the world and will pit their new discipleship against worldly modes of life. The gospel transforms, rather than primarily seeking to interpret.

Moreover such claims are public and universal. They are not private truth, not gnostic and to be kept hidden. This truth is cosmic in scope: Christ died and rose; the Church is a new humanity, not an interest group with a secret doctrine to be kept away from the public gaze. The gospel has relevance for the human condition, or it is nothing.[26] The Church should be prepared to speak its sole message in dialogue with society. The strategy of privatising church teaching, rendering it purely 'in-house' and of no interest to all humanity, negates not only the New Testament but the patristic commitments of the Church of England. The current strategy, adopted by the Boards of the Church of England, in education and social policy for example, of forgetting that the Church is the Church of Jesus Christ, on the grounds of pluralism and unbelief in society, can only be regarded as an inversion of the classical Irenaean ethos.

'The elimination of all features of a world-view from Christian conceptions of faith', says Pannenberg, 'was matched positively by the limitation of faith to the subjectivity of existential self-understanding. That is where the assimilation to the spirit of secular culture lies, for the subjectivity of the private individual is precisely the place which secular culture gives to religion while disputing all its claims that its statements have objective truth'.[27] The church's collusion with this secularising agenda has resulted in real damage to the nation and the church.

The 1944 Education Act, for example, and the church's handing over of so much of its influence to the state, resulted in a dramatic decline of Christian influence. Further, those schools which did remain in Church of England control were left to drift; no plan for sustaining Christian ethos was developed, despite the existence of the then 'church' colleges. Hastings, the leading historian of the period, tells us, 'The quickly advancing secular consensus of middle England in the sixties owed a great deal to the educational choices made in the 1940s.[28]

These were choices made by churchmen, and are followed vigorously today.[29] Indeed the benefits of relativism and plurality of all faiths, none being taken as more true than others, is distinctive of Church of England religious educationalists now. Anglican educational advisors attacked Baroness Cox's legislation giving the Christian faith a focal place in the RE curriculum, a testimony to the power of this relativist policy. The Irenaean message of public christological truth, true for all or for none, has proved too embarrassing for Anglican bureaucracy.

The same verdict applies to the withdrawal of the Church of England's voice and place from the field of health policy. Its voice on the multitude of abortions carried out in the United Kingdom is not heard. Chaplaincies are mutating into humanistic counselling agencies.[30] The strongly vocational basis of British nursing has been allowed to die wholly unnoticed by the church, which could have set up distinctive tracks of training in its colleges, with appropriate supporting ethical studies. Faith is regarded as wholly private, irrelevant to professional life, even for the caring professions.

A church which allows itself to dilute its message, to step away from or bracket its christological centre, will not long remain a church, and paradoxically will cease to be of interest to pagan or secular society as its voice becomes merged into that of a general humanism. Irenaeus was right; God is the God of all creation, relevant to all human concerns. The gospel is public truth, not to be subjectivised. If one function of establishment is to reinforce this retreat into the inner, private spirituality, then it is a major argument for disestablishment. The doctrinal and ethical base of the church stems from this gospel fact; she dies, and fails everyone, if she drifts away into secular ideology, out of her christological orbit.

Notes

1. The 'Preface' to *Crockford's Clerical Directory* 1978/8 (Church House Publishing, London, 1987).
2. Tom Oden, *Agenda for Theology: After Modernity What?* (Zondervan, Grand Rapids, 1992).
3. ibid., p. 50.
4. ibid.
5. In *God in Us*, (SCM, London, 1993) Anthony Freeman argued for atheistic Christian humanism and, after a time for reflection allowed by his bishop, had his licence revoked.
6. *Issues in Human Sexuality: A Statement by the House of Bishops of the General Synod of the Church of England* (Church House Publishing, London, 1991).
7. J. H. Newman, Appendix to *Apologia Pro Vita Sua* (1865 edn.) (Oxford University Press, Oxford, 1913), p. 396.
8. ibid.
9. Clifford Longley, 'Becoming a National Church', a paper given to the Roman Catholic Bishops' Conference of England and Wales, 1993.
10. ibid. p. 17. Because of this Longley thinks 'the Roman Catholic Church's mission to the nation must change. It has now to shoulder a greater share of the national burden; and may yet find itself ... taking over the leadership'.
11. Grace Davie, in her *Religion in Britain since 1945; Believing Without Belonging* (Blackwell, Oxford, 1994), shows the complexity of labelling British society 'secular' without considerable qualification and nuancing.
12. 'To the extent that a religion is subversive of the society in which it is practised and divides that society, Durkheim's sociology of religion remains unable to cope with it', Lewis A. Coser, 'Durkheim's Conservatism', in *Essays on Sociology and Philosophy*, ed. Kurt H. Wolff (Harper Torchbooks, New York, 1964), p. 226.
13. Oliver O'Donovan, *Resurrection and Moral Order* (IVP, Leicester, 1968), p. 20.
14. There is a debate to be had about the self-understanding of society as non-Christian. Opinion polls stubbornly represent this self-understanding as Christian to a consistent 70%. This no doubt represents a fairly 'nominal' Christian self-understanding of a 'cultural Christianity', but it is precisely the culture, or the national 'secular' ethos, that is in question here: society thinks of itself as in the Christian moral tradition – the Church of England boards and committees insist on contradicting this and labelling society more secular than it wishes to be labelled.
15. K. Barth, *Church Dogmatics* vol I/1 (T & T Clark, Edinburgh, 2nd edn., 1975), p. 55.

16. The decade of evangelism, in the British context, might well have emphasised the renewal of an existing, but faded, faith as much as the creation of completely new faith.

17. A. M. Ramsey, *God, Christ and the World* (SCM, London, 1969).

18. For a recent affirmation of this Augustinian position see *Salvation and the Church. An Agreed Statement by the Second Anglican–Roman Catholic International Commission* (Church House Publishing & Catholic Truth Society, London, 1987).

19. *Church as Communion. An Agreed Statement by the Second Anglican–Roman Catholic International Commission* (Church House Publishing & Catholic Truth Society, London, 1991), p. 13.

20. eg., A. Dulles, *The Catholicity of the Church*, (Clarendon Press, Oxford, 1985), p. 40.

21. S. Sykes, *The Identity of Christianity* (SPCK, London, 1984), pp. 35ff., sets out this view.

22. *Ecclesiastical Polity* Book 3, ch. i.9.

23. eg., *From Gore to Temple* (Longmans, London, 1960), p. 175ff.

24. S. Hall, *Doctrine and Practice in the Early Church* (SPCK, London, 1991), p. 60, summarises Irenaeus's view.

25. *Faith in the City: The Report of the Archbishop of Canterbury's Commission on Urban Priority Areas* (Church House Publishing, London, 1985).

26. Not only is this protest about privatisation heard from the well-known *Gospel and Culture* movement led by Bishop Lesslie Newbigin, but Pannenberg's powerful voice can also be adduced in its favour: God is the God of all reality, not of a gnostic segment. See eg. W. Pannenberg, *Systematic Theology* vol. I (T & T Clark, Edinburgh, 1991) and *Christianity in a Secularized World* (SCM, London, 1989).

27. W. Pannenberg, *Christianity in a Secularized World*, p. 51.

28. Adrian Hastings, *A History of English Christianity 1920–1990* (SCM, London, 1991), p. 421.

29. Hastings quotes R.A. Butler, the author of the 1944 Education Act, twenty years after the Act: 'the perfunctory and uninspired nature of the religious instruction provided in all too many local authority and controlled schools had begun ... to imperil the Christian basis of society.' ibid.

30. See, eg., David Stoter, *Spiritual Aspects of Health Care* (Mosby, London, 1995). Written by a hospital chaplain, this book articulates a definition of an anthropocentric spiritual dimension, bracketing religion as part of this need, and with barely any reference to Christianity. Psychological and aesthetic analyses of spirituality form its basis.

Cyprianus Anglicus:
St Cyprian and the Future
of Anglicanism

Mark D. Chapman

It is no accident that Peter Heylyn gave his polemical biography of Archbishop Laud the title *Cyprianus Anglicus*,[1] since it has been St Cyprian, perhaps more than any other Father, who has provided the basis for the authority claimed by the Anglican Church.[2] By looking at the use made of Cyprian, mainly by a number of English bishops and archbishops, this paper seeks to trace the growth of the sort of authority claimed by Anglicanism from its beginnings which is manifested in the defence of archiepiscopal and provincial rights against both Rome and Puritan alike. Cyprian's example was used, on the one hand, to defend the rights of each province to autonomy against the authority of any extra-provincial bishop, and, on the other hand, to defend archiepiscopal rights against those of lesser bishops and other clergy and, most particularly, against the puritan claim of the equality of all orders of ministry. It is the contention of this paper that, even though Cyprian's authority in other matters may be highly questionable,[3] there may be some mileage yet in a doctrine of provincial autonomy developed from his writings.[4]

I. The Background in Cyprian

Though Cyprian is cited frequently by the English Reformers and by the Anglican writers of the seventeenth century in relation both to the sacraments and to the sacerdotal authority of the priesthood, his particular relevance to the problem of authority in Anglicanism is to be found chiefly in his responses to the conflicts surrounding various schisms in Carthage and Rome. These debates have been well-rehearsed elsewhere,[5] but what has been of utmost importance in Anglican interpretation is Cyprian's treatise in response to schism, *On the Unity of the Catholic Church*, where he claimed that nothing could excuse the sin of division, since the church, epitomised by the office of the episcopate, is one (i.e. unique) and the unity of the church is to be found in the mutual recognition of bishops. Similarly, any alternative authority to that of the single bishop in each diocese (in this case that of the 'confessor') was denied.[6] For Cyprian no particular bishop, including the Roman Pope,[7] had absolute authority. Instead all bishops collectively shared the authority granted to Peter and together they formed a college.

Relations between Cyprian and Rome grew most difficult over the question of the validity of baptism outside the fold. For Cyprian, those who had been baptized out of unity with the Catholic Church were to be treated on the same basis as the pagan and would have to be rebaptized.[8] Pope Stephen, however, regarded baptism as valid even when it was performed by those outside the Church since it depended primarily on the faith of the believer,[9] which led him to denounce Cyprian as a 'false Christ'.[10] In turn, Stephen's assertion of Roman primacy led Cyprian to convene a Council at Carthage where he reasserted the right of all bishops to decide for themselves in consultation and dialogue with other bishops.[11] In this Cyprian laid the grounds for a doctrine of provincial autonomy which was to be greatly developed in Anglican theology.

II. Jewel, Laud and the Authority of Rome

Though admittedly no constructive thinker,[12] Archbishop Laud, 'caught betwixt Popery and Schism,' set out to defend 'the Protestant Cause with his Pen',[13] attempting to show that, although outside the church there was no salvation, nevertheless '[t]he Catholic Church is neither Rome, nor a conventicle'.[14] In his *Conference* with Fisher he begins and ends with a lengthy exposition of St Cyprian. In this he is following Jewel, who, also in dialogue with a Roman Catholic, Harding, cites Cyprian, claiming that 'the authority of the bishops in Africa is as good as that authority of the bishop of Rome'[15] and that there can be no appeal to Rome from the provincial bishop, since this was a 'hindrance of right'.[16]

Laud develops this further by claiming that the authority of the patriarch of Rome is essentially the same as that of the other patriarchs, each of whom, including the archbishop of Canterbury,[17] is 'supreme in his own patriarchate'.[18] There is thus no sense in which

Laud wishes to unchurch the Church of Rome for failing to reform itself,[19] but instead he seeks to ensure that there are legitimate spheres of action for each provincial church which together form the universal Church.[20]

Laud, like Jewel, is therefore keen to emphasise that no one part of the Church, especially the Church of Rome, is free from error;[21] indeed virtually the whole of the *Conference* is concerned with the possibility of ecclesiastical error. It was not so much that the Pope had erred, but rather he had no particular right merely in virtue of his office to claim exemption from all error. Consequently, Laud goes on, the only proper way of deciding whether Cyprian or Stephen, or any other had erred was to convene a council of bishops. However, Laud was also clear that even such general councils of bishops could err[22] because 'if a General Council will go out of the Church's way, it may easily go without the Church's truth'.[23] Similarly Jewel had earlier claimed that Councils cannot make a rule of faith nor bind anybody's faith:[24] indeed 'Tertullian, Cyprian, Clemens Alexandrinus ... were oftentimes much deceived'.[25] Though claiming indefectibility,[26] Laud adds that this is not identical to the decisions of General Councils: the Catholic Church was far greater and more expansive. Indeed the only authority 'of divine and infallible verity' is Scripture which also tests the pronouncements of general councils.[27] Indeed Laud cites Cyprian to show that the authority of councils derives from the practical need to settle disputes, and was consequently ad hoc and provisional.

At the same time, Cyprian is also used by Laud to show that the individual province is often forced to make decisions for itself because of the impossibility of ever convening a general council. While admitting that decisions of autonomous provincial synods are provisional, Laud nevertheless held that they are necessary stopgaps until such time as proper general councils can be convened. Thus when a general council 'cannot be had, the church must pray that it may, and expect till it may; or else reform itself *per partes*, by national or provincial synods'.[28] It is crucial that, where the general Church refuses to reform itself, the particular must set about this task. Thus Laud asked: 'Was it not lawful for Judah to reform herself when Israel would not join? Sure it was, or else the prophet deceives me?'.[29] A few pages on Laud's language became somewhat more graphic: 'Should we have suffered this gangrene to endanger life and all rather than be cured in time by a physician of a weaker knowledge and a less able hand?'.[30] Indeed he claims that there would have been no general councils had not provincial synods set about the reforming task beforehand. In short, he maintains, 'when the universal Church will not, or for the iniquities of the times cannot, obtain and settle a free General Council, it is lawful, nay sometimes necessary, to reform gross abuses by a national, or a provincial'.[31]

Laud lists a number of provincial councils which have acted on their own authority[32] and 'if,' he writes, 'this were practised so often, and in so many places, why may not a National Council of the Church of England do the like? -as she did'.[33] In this he is following Jewel, who made the similar claim that 'the truth of God'[34] was more important than the forum of decision making. Thus provincial councils have reformed the 'vanities and unseemly follies' but have done nothing which touches on the truth of the Christian faith.

By extension, the function of bishops, according to Laud, was to provide a system of voluntary practical checks and balances against the authority of the Church of Rome with its one viceroy.[35] Episcopal authority thus involves a willingness to share decision making and to submit to the authority of the whole Church while at the same time retaining the possibility of removing assent where this whole was in error. Thus even when the bishops were assembled together there was always the further test of Scripture which gave to the province the possibility of unilateral action in order to rectify something blatantly in error.[36]

III. Whitgift, Hooker and the Authority of the Primate

Since they were writing against Roman Catholic opponents neither Jewel nor Laud felt any particular need to justify the authority of bishops. Others, most importantly John Whitgift and Richard Hooker, however, had to set about justifying the power of archbishops over their provinces in response to the understanding of the equality of orders maintained by their Puritan opponents.[37] In doing so, both were to make extensive use of Cyprian. Thus Whitgift claims against Cartwright that the equality of bishops is in fact the equality of *arch-bishops*, who alone provided a proper focus of unity in each place.[38] For Whitgift and for Hooker,[39] the archbishop is superior to other pastors and is thus 'chief over his own province and not subject to any. The bishop of Rome had no jurisdiction over the bishop of Carthage, but they were of equal power and authority; as others also were of the like seats'.[40]

According to Whitgift it was quite absurd to leave the judgement of the heretic solely to Christ: there had to be a prior judgement on earth. Thus Cyprian's claim that 'no one of us setteth himself up as a bishop of bishops' was against rule by tyranny,[41] but not against decent order in the Church.[42] Indeed the metropolitan still had the duty to intervene in certain cases.[43] In short, the duty of the arch-bishop was to 'keep the peace'.[44] Similarly, although Hooker claims a greater degree of collegiality and asserts that 'amongst the African bishops none did use such authority over any as the bishop of Rome did afterward claim over all,'[45] he agrees with Whitgift as to the legal and pragmatic functions of the archbishop in managing conflict.[46]

From this discussion of provincial and primatial authority in clas-sical Anglican theology, three clear points emerge. Firstly, there was a legitimate sphere of action for the province to initiate reform where the general Church would not act, in the hope that this would in turn influence the wider Church. Secondly, even where the general Church could act it was nevertheless capable of erring since it too was trying to make little more than pragmatic decisions to resolve particular prob-lems. Thirdly, the authority of the province, of archbishops and of synods was limited in most matters to the pragmatic function of solving disputes and conflicts when they arose. It was a necessary though limited authority which was to ensure a proper and decent order in the Church in which all could live together in a not always easy peace.

IV. Archbishop Benson and the Reassertion of Cyprianic Authority.

Though the pioneer ecumenist, Archbishop Wake, reaffirmed the Cyprianic dictum that 'the chair of Peter ... is preserved in all Catholic Churches,'[47] and although Cyprian was used in the arguments about episcopacy in Scotland, as well as during the non-juring schism,[48] it was only with the expansion of the Anglican Church over-seas and the development of Lambeth Conferences that both provincial autonomy and pragmatic responsive authority once again came to be of vital importance.[49] In this it was Archbishop Benson more than anyone else who sought theological inspiration from St Cyprian in responding to the question: 'What provision has the Mother Church made to adjust its relations with its children as they grow up to adoles-cence and maturity?'[50]

In his *magnum opus* on Cyprian Benson emphasises the collegial-ity of the bishops 'advising by mutual consent, yet not even when unanimous constraining a single dissentient bishop'.[51] In this Benson follows a similar path to Laud and remarks that the unity of the bishops was not an infallible unity, but a practical unity, a moral unity, held together by its own sense of unity, by 'the cement of mutual concord'. As problems arose they were to consider them each by itself. The first thing was that they should, with as deliberate consultation as could be had, state their several opinions without fear or favour.[52]

There was thus a kind of democracy between bishops. Cyprianic unity arose from a mutual respect between all bishops in the practical need to settle disputes as they occurred: it was thus neither a coerced unity nor a legalistic authority. Instead a bishop was free to disobey, and if he did, he was 'unassailable unless viciousness or false doctrine were patent in his life or teaching'.[53]

There was obvious relevance in this for the development of the Lambeth Conference. Presiding over it in 1888 Benson reminded the assembled bishops that though the gospel was something which transcended time and place and thereby put all merely local customs into perspective, each province had nevertheless to respond to these customs.[54] Similarly in a sermon preached the year before at the consecration of Truro Cathedral, Benson maintained that the unity desired by the church did not imply uniformity[55] but was a goal.[56] In reaching this goal there had to be some 'elasticity' as new situations produced different responses.[57] New provincial churches were consequently not to be ruled directly from England but were to be allowed to develop 'churches truly native' as the gospel responded to new needs and new situations.[58] Indeed, a failure to be responsive to the cultural conditions and 'to seek to build up a like Church ... out of the utterly different characters, experiences, sentiments of another race, is to repeat without excuse the error of the great Boniface, in making not a Teutonic but an Italian Church in Germany. It is to contradict the wise axioms with which Gregory tried to save Augustine from the error'.[59]

V. William Temple: the Breadth of Catholicity.

Drawing on the same Cyprianic tradition, William Temple similarly emphasised the unity of the episcopate but saw it as a sacramental expression of Christ's 'one truth'.[60] Such unity, however, did not imply uniformity, but was a 'socialist' unity, 'where the single life of the whole absolutely depends on the diversity of the parts alike in form and function'.[61] The fulness of Christ's unity was beyond any temporal expression and could only be hinted at in the huge diversity of humanity. Consequently Christian unity already existed, not as some artificial visible unity between diverse bodies but as a 'fellowship of men, each of whom Christ has united with himself'.[62] Unity depended not so much on an outward and visible union as on a shared faith: shared order was therefore 'not essential at all'. Temple thus developed the Cyprianic understanding of unity, which had depended originally very much on the one visible episcopate shared in by all bishops, into a vision of the ultimate truth, of the true Church, which served to relativize all partial attempts to give voice to this truth.[63] Cyprianic unity has here been transferred to a hidden future; all visible churches are but frail and feeble attempts to express this future truth, but each limited to its 'provincial' context.

VI. Michael Ramsey

Drawing more explicitly from Cyprian, Michael Ramsey, in *The Gospel and the Catholic Church*,[64] attempted to provide a coherent basis for the authority claimed by the Church of England. Although he recognises that Cyprian was 'rigid', he also claims that his understanding of the episcopate emerged from a view where a divided Church 'was a monstrous impossibility'.[65] However, it was wrong to see the episcopate as bearing the whole weight of the unity of the Church: the first fact ought instead to be the 'Church's corporate family life'. The episcopate ought thus to function as an expression of that whole life.[66] Thus Ramsey points to 'a reunited Church wherein the truths seen in every section of christendom must be preserved in full measure, wherein there will be a variety of type and form, but wherein the organ of unity will be the one episcopate, *never* because it is Anglican, *always* because it belongs to the whole family of God'.

Indeed in a striking passage Ramsey emphasises the ecumenical role of the Anglican Church as that of pointing to the very provisionality, the fragmentary character of any visible church. Its most important credentials are 'its incompleteness, with the tension and the travail in its soul. It is clumsy and untidy, it baffles neatness and logic'. And yet Ramsey identifies this recognition of the limited character of any church with catholicism itself, as the 'means of deliverance into the Gospel of God and the timeless Church... For it frees [the thoughtful Christian] from partial rationalisms ... and it delivers him into an orthodoxy which no individual and no group can possess'.[67]

VII. Federalised Authority: a Cyprianic Understanding of Catholicity

In this development by Benson, Temple and Ramsey of a Cyprianic understanding of unity to embrace such an invisible and even eschatological criterion of unity, there is a (perhaps surprising) similarity to Archbishop Laud who refused to delimit the boundaries of catholicity, but who instead desired 'to open those wider gates of the Catholic Church, confined to no age, time or place'.[68] The sole criterion of catholicity is the preaching and teaching of the catholic faith as tested by Scripture.

Anglican interpretations of Cyprianic ideas thus moved away from the idea of the monarchical bishop ruling in his province, towards the exercise of an authority which humbly and cautiously reacted to problems as they arose: authority was indeed something to be used as seldom as possible. As Benson clearly recognised, there could only ever be diverse Christian communities responding to their cultural situations: all authority had thus to be relative to this particular local context. Similarly, there could be no monolithic unitary Church, since all authority was based on the living authority of those who placed their allegiance in a particular church.

Perhaps the most coherent theorist of this 'federalised'[69] Church was J.N. Figgis,[70] who held that 'there is in the universe [no] authority rigidly absolute... The truth rather sees the spirit of Christ, the authority in the Christian body as a whole, and does not concentrate it in a centre, not even in a general council. In every organic part of it there is the Church'.[71] The universal Church, in so far as it existed at all, was very much a body which depended for its authority on the groups which comprised it, and who conceded to it a specific realm for adjudication in disputes. Admittedly, Figgis claimed, this did not 'give us the clear-cut logical system of Rome; but it has the realism, the variety, the richness, the infinite powers of growth and adaptability of life itself'.[72] The group of groups, the catholic Church, was thus highly flexible and disorganised.

In this understanding of catholicity, Figgis respected the sort of constitution which was beginning to develop within the Anglican communion. All authority had ultimately to rest with the living parts of the Church, the worshipping communities, and any wider, extra-provincial authority was parasitic upon this. Consequently he maintained a very practical and pragmatic vision of the Church catholic as something always in flux as new insights and a changing perspective engendered new experiments and new ideas. Thus

[t]he theory on which the English Church ... bases its doctrine is the direct opposite [of the ultramontane theory where all authority is gathered at the centre]. The authority of the Church is ... a synthesis of all the living parts of the Church... Any universal constitution to which we might approach, would be ultimately of the federalist type.[73]

Figgis thus brings the Cyprianic vision to its clearest expression as the basis for the authority of the Anglican communion as that of a humble, provisional church ever hoping to express something of the gospel of Christ, looking for its authority from beyond history, but nevertheless always forced to compromise with time and place.[74] The Church *is* one because Christ is one (as symbolised sacramentally by the episcopate), and yet it is diverse and manifold because it is always historical. This fact should lead any theorist of ecclesiastical authority to recognise at least some degree of relativity in any provincial expression of Christianity. It requires a degree of humility, revealed by so many occupants of the chair of Augustine, to see the triumphs of any provincial church as always partial and provisional, simply because they are always provincial. The oneness of the gospel of Christ, so clearly recognised by Ramsey, stands over against any limited ecclesiastical construct, however glorious.[75]

It might thus be said that, whatever its inelegance and inherent instability, Cyprian's ecclesiology as developed in Anglicanism is perhaps a better starting point for an ecclesiology than any conceivable alternative, for rigidity without 'suppleness and elasticity'[76] leads inexorably either to schism or to a coercive authoritarianism which ultimately denies human diversity. It must be said, however, as was recognised by the Lambeth Conference of 1948, 'that authority of this kind is much harder to understand and obey than anything of a more imperious character'. Despite this, however, the bishops went on to claim that it was nevertheless 'true and we glory in the appeal it makes to faith'.[77] And surely, one would want to affirm, when it comes to the future of Anglicanism, it is this humble lack of imperiousness that needs to be borne in mind in any attempt to erect a new 'house of authority'.

Notes

1. Peter Heylyn, *Cyprianus Anglicus or, The History of the Life and Death of the Most Revered and Renowned Prelate William, by Divine Providence, Lord Archbishop of Canterbury* (A. Seile, London, 1668).
2. Though other archbishops may not have shared Cyprian's fate, many have

been equally indebted to him. Archbishop Benson, for instance, is described by his son and biographer as quite obsessional in his interest. cf. A. C. Benson, introduction to E. W. Benson, *Cyprian His Life. His Times. His Work* (Macmillan, London, 1897), p.iv; cf. A. C. Benson, *The Life of Edward White Benson* (Macmillan, London, 1900), 2 Vols, Vol.II, p.707.

3. cf. Maurice Wiles, 'The Theological Legacy of St. Cyprian', *Journal of Ecclesiastical History* 14 (1963), pp.139-149.

4. On this, see my essay, 'Catholicity, Unity and Provincial Autonomy: On Making Decisions Unilaterally', *Anglican Theological Review* 76 (1994), pp.313-328. Another recent attempt to apply Cyprianic theology to contemporary Anglicanism has been made by John C. Bauerschmidt in 'Cyprian, Augustine, and the *Pars Donati*: Reflections on the Eames Commission and the Fort Worth Synod', *Saint Luke's Journal of Theology* 34 (1991), pp.1-16.

5. e.g. by Stuart G. Hall, *Doctrine and Practice in the Early Church* (SPCK, London, 1991), Chapter 9. On Cyprian, see Peter Hinchliff, *Cyprian of Carthage and the Unity of the Catholic Church* (Geoffrey Chapman, London, 1974); and M.M. Sage, *Cyprian* (Philadelphia Patristic Foundation, Cambridge, Mass, 1975); M. Bévenot, Article on Cyprian in *TRE* 8 (1981), pp.246-54.

6. *De Catholicae Ecclesiae Unitate* §5. One of the most important early editions of Cyprian was prepared by Bishops Fell and Pearson in 1682. An important English translation was *The Treatises of S. Caecilius Cyprian* in *A Library of the Fathers*, (Parker, Oxford, 1876). The relevant passage is found on p.134. A more recent translation was made by M. Bévenot (*Oxford Early Christian Texts*, Oxford, 1971). This crucial passage is cited frequently in interpreters from John Jewel to Michael Ramsey.

7. At least on Anglican readings which opposed the variant 'Primacy' reading in §§4 and 5 which traced apostolic succession solely to the 'chair' of Peter and consequently to Rome. On the variant readings of *De Unitate* see esp. M. Bévenot, *The Tradition of Manuscripts: A Study in the Transmission of St Cyprian's Treatises* (Oxford University Press, Oxford, 1961). Though the Primacy version may well be authentic it merely represents an 'occasional concession, dictated by tactical considerations, since it contradicts Cyprian's view as clearly formulated elsewhere' (Hans von Campenhausen, *Ecclesiastical Authority and Spiritual Power in the Church of the First Three Centuries* (A & C Black, London, 1969), p.276).

8. *Epp.* 73.3, 74.5. English translations in *The Letters of St Cyprian*, tr. G.W. Clarke (Newman Press, New York, 1986).

9. cf. *Epp.* 75.18, 20; 73.14.

10. *Ep.* 75.25.

11. cf. Cyprian's speech at the Seventh Council of Carthage, Sept. 1st, AD 256, §87 in *Library of the Fathers* xvii. 286ff. On this Council see Joseph Fischer, 'Das Konzil zu Karthago im Spätsommer 256', *Annuarium*

Historiae Conciliorum 16 (1984) pp.1-39. Cyprian's monarchical authority has recently been re-evaluated in terms of his close relationship with
the whole body of believers. See esp. J. Partout Burns, 'On Rebaptism.
Social Organisation in the 3rd Century Church', *Journal of Early
Christian Studies* 1 (1993), p.367-403. The degree of unanimity between
the bishops attending the Council has also recently been closely investi-
gated. It seems that the Council was rather more collegial and less
monarchical than is often supposed. See esp. Enrique Contreras,
'Sententiae Episcoporum Numero LXXXVII de Haereticis Baptizandis',
Augustinianum 27 (1987), pp.407-425, and J.J. Sebastian, 'Mere Rubber
Stamps? The Voting Pattern of the Bishops at the Council of Carthage
on 1 September 256' (Unpublished paper delivered at the 12th
International Conference on Patristic Studies, Oxford 1995).

12. cf. E.C.E. Bourne, *The Anglicanism of William Laud* (SPCK, London,
    1947), Chapter 4.
13. Heylyn, op. cit., p.3.
14. 'A Relation of the Conference between William Laud and Mr. Fisher the
    Jesuit' in *Works (Library of Anglo-Catholic Theology)* (Parker, Oxford,
    1849), Vol.II, p.xvii. H.R. McAdoo describes this work as representing
    the 'Anglican average since its author, though historically a most signif-
    icant figure and obviously widely read in theology, particularly in
    patristic studies, was not a leading theologian of the day' ('The Influence
    of the Seventeenth Century on Contemporary Anglican Understanding of
    the Purpose and Functioning of Authority in the Church' in *Christian
    Authority. Essays in Honour of Henry Chadwick*, ed. G.R. Evans
    (Clarendon Press, Oxford, 1988), Chapter Thirteen, p.267).
15. References are to the *Parker Society* edition, *The Works of John Jewel*
    (Cambridge University Press, Cambridge, 1848), Vol. III, pp.284, 300;
    cf. Vol.IV, p.1119; Vol.II, p.1001.
16. Jewel, op. cit., Vol.I, p.388; Vol.III, p.300.
17. Laud, op. cit., p.190. It is, however, hard to imagine some archbishops
    of Canterbury as possessing patriarchal status.
18. ibid., p.189.
19. ibid., p.314. Though Laud regarded Rome as a true church, his opinion
    of it was hardly high. Cf. Heylyn, op.cit, p.19: 'Just as a man distem-
    pered in his Brain, diseased in all the parts of his body, and languishing
    under many putrefied sores, doth still retain the being of natural man as
    long as he has sense and motion and (in his lucid moments) some use
    of reason'.
20. Laud, op. cit., p.410.
21. ibid., p.8f. cf. p.404.
22. ibid., p.247.
23. ibid., p.266.
24. Jewel, op. cit., Vol.II, p.996.
25. ibid., Vol.III, p.176f.
26. Laud, op. cit., p.366. Laud is here repeating the argument of Article
    XXI: 'When [General Councils] be gathered together, (forasmuch as they

be an assembly of men, whereof all be not governed with the Spirit and Word of God,) they may err, and sometimes have erred, even in things pertaining unto God. Wherefore things ordained by them as necessary to salvation have neither strength nor authority, unless it may be declared that they be taken out of Holy Scripture'. On this, see H.R. McAdoo, op. cit., esp. p.258.

27. Laud, op. cit., p.218. Heylyn comments that Laud had no regard for Luther or Calvin but 'only to the prophets and the apostles' (op. cit., p.3).

28. Laud, op. cit., p.235.

29. ibid., p.167f.

30. ibid., p.170.

31. ibid., p.170. To justify his claim about the priority of national and provincial reform he draws on the schoolman Albertus Magnus (*c*.1200-1280) (II, p.168), as well as the Parisian Professor and conciliar theorist, Jean Gerson (1363-1429), who 'will not deny but that the Church may be reformed in parts; and that this is necessary, and that to effect it, Provincial Councils may suffice; and in some things, Diocesan' (ibid.).

32. ibid., p.171.

33. ibid., p.172.

34. Jewel, op. cit., Vol.IV, p.1053f.

35. Laud, op. cit., p.225.

36. Some centuries later, the Anglican Newman gave similar arguments in 'The Catholicity of the Anglican Church' (1840) where he stated: 'Each diocese is a perfect independent church, sufficient for itself; and the communion of Christians one with another, and the unity of them all together, lie ... not in what they do in common ... but in what they are and what they have in common, in their possession of the Succession... [T]he Church is complete in one bishopric; a number of bishoprics are but reiterations of one, and add nothing to the perfection of the system. As there is one Bishop invisible in heaven, so there is but one bishop on earth; and the multitude of bishops are ... one and all shadows and organs of one and the same divine reality' (J.H. Newman, *Essays Critical and Historical* (Basil Montagu Pickering, London, 18733), Vol.II. pp.20, 23). For Newman at this stage all bishops represented the unity of the Church in sharing in one universal episcopate, and although they might possess a difference of rank, their authority was one and the same, and was identical to the authority of the catholic Church in which they shared. What seems lacking in Newman, however, is the wider vision of catholicity, part of which must always be invisible and which Laud still retained.

37. See esp. Richard Hooker, *Ecclesiastical Polity*, eds. Keble, Church and Paget (Oxford University Press, Oxford, 1888), Bk.VII.xiii.2.

38. References are to the *Parker Society* edition: *The Works of John Whitgift* (Cambridge University Press, Cambridge, 1851), 3 Vols, here Vol.II, p.200. Hooker recites almost identical arguments.

39. Hooker, op. cit., Bk.VII.xvi.6. Citing Cyprian, *Ep*.69.

40. Whitgift, op. cit., Vol.II, p.207, citing *Ep*.66: 'But which of us is far from humility, I, who daily serve the brethren, and with kindness and joy receive all that come to the church, or you who set yourself up as a bishop of a bishop, and as a judge of the judge for the time appointed by God?' (§2). cf. Hooker, op. cit., Bk.VII.xiii.2: 'Cyprian being bishop of Carthage was clearly superior unto all other ministers there; yea Cyprian was by reason of the dignity of his see an archbishop, and so consequently superior unto bishops'.
41. Whitgift, op. cit., Vol.II, pp.209, 212.
42. ibid., p.209.
43. ibid., p.209.
44. ibid., p.210.
45. Hooker, op. cit., Bk.VII.xvi.7.
46. ibid., Bk.VII.xvi.8.
47. Cited in Norman Sykes, *William Wake* (Cambridge University Press, Cambridge, 1957), Vol.I, p.274.
48. The interpretation of Cyprian is particularly important in the dispute between the Scottish non-juring Bishop, John Sage, Gilbert Rule, Principal of Edinburgh University and the controversialist William Jameson in the first years of the eighteenth century. See esp. John Sage, *The Principles of the Cyprianic Age, with regard to episcopal power and jurisdiction, asserted from the writings of St Cyprian himself, by which it is made evident that the Vindicator of the Kirk of Scotland is obliged by his own concessions to acknowledge that he and his associates are schismaticks* (London 1695); John Sage, *A Vindication of a discourse entitled The Principles of the Cyprianic Age – reply to G. Rule's Cyprianic bishop examined and found not to be a diocesan (*London 1701)*;* William Jameson, *Cyprianus Isotimus, or John Sage's Vindication of his Principles of the Cyprianic Age confuted* (Edinburgh 1705).
49. cf. G.R. Evans, *Authority in the Church: A Challenge for Anglicans* (Canterbury Press, Norwich, 1990), esp. Chapter Five.
50. Cited in J. McLeod Campbell, *Christian History in the Making* (The Press and Publications Board of the Church Assembly, London, 1946), p.320.
51. E.W. Benson, op. cit., p.190.
52. ibid., p.195.
53. ibid., p.195.
54. As Bishop of Truro, Benson had already demonstrated this principle and had zealously attempted to grow acquainted with the history and peculiarities of the Duchy of Cornwall. cf. A.C. Benson, op. cit., Vol.I, p.428.
55. 'Growing Unity' in Edward White Benson, *Living Theology* (Sampson Low, Marston and Co., London, 1893), pp.131-145, here p.139.
56. ibid., p.133.
57. 'New-Born Churches' in *Living Theology*, pp.111-127, here p.117.
58. Cited in A.C. Benson, op. cit., Vol.II, p.466.
59. Visitation Charge of 1885 in A.C. Benson, op. cit., Vol.II, p.465f.

60. 'The Church' in *Foundations. A Statement of Christian Belief in Terms of Modern Thought*, ed. B. H. Streeter (Macmillan, London, 1912), p.343. cf. p.347.
61. ibid., p.349.
62. *Religious Experience* (James Clarke, London, 1958), p.21.
63. *Christus Veritas* (Macmillan, London, 1924), p.167f.
64. (Longmans, London, 1936). *De unitate* §4f is cited on p.150f.
65. Ramsey, op. cit., p.151.
66. ibid., p.152.
67. ibid., p.135.
68. Laud, op. cit., Vol.II, p.xviif.
69. J.N. Figgis, *Hopes for English Religion* (Longmans, London, 1919), p.80.
70. On Figgis, see my essay, 'Concepts of the Voluntary Church in England and Germany, 1890-1920: A Study of J.N. Figgis and Ernst Troeltsch' *Zeitschrift für neuere Theologiegeschichte* 2 (1995), pp.37-59. cf. Maurice G. Tucker, *John Neville Figgis. A Study* (SPCK, London, 1950).
71. *The Fellowship of the Mystery* (Longmans, London, 1914), p.202.
72. *Hopes for English Religion*, p.80.
73. J.N. Figgis, *Churches in the Modern State* (Longmans, London, 1914), p.166.
74. The Report of the 1948 Lambeth Conference summarised this dilemma which rests at the heart of ecclesial authority: 'Authority, as inherited by the Anglican communion from the undivided Church of the early centuries of the Christian era, is single in that it is derived from a single Divine source, and reflects within itself the richness and historicity of the divine Revelation' (*The Lambeth Conference 1948* (SPCK, London, 1948), p.84f). This historicity means that it is also a 'dispersed rather than a centralized authority, having many elements which combine, inter-act with, and check each other'.
75. cf. R.P.C. Hanson, *Tradition in the Early Church* (SCM, London, 1962), p.156: 'Cyprian held most passionately that it was a gravely wrong policy to admit heretics to the Church without rebaptizing them; but he was prepared to allow Stephen to continue in what was, in Cyprian's eyes, a disastrously false custom. Modern theologians who find it difficult to envisage reunion with people of different ecclesiastical traditions would do well to consider this'.
76. *Lambeth 1948*, p.85.
77. ibid., p.85.

Antiquity as a Guide to Orthodoxy? A Critical Appraisal of Newman's *Via Media*

Kenneth A. Locke

Introduction

This paper takes a critical look at the idea of Anglican orthodoxy and authority defended by the Oxford Movement, and in particular by John Henry Newman, in the earlier half of the nineteenth century.[1] My choice of the Oxford Movement is not arbitrary. I am concerned with assessing the theological significance of its appeal to antiquity, because the Tractarians', and especially Newman's, articulation of the appeal to antiquity has been viewed as paradigmatic by later Anglican ecclesiologists. Indeed, one hundred years after its initiation Frank Leslie Cross could comment that the Tractarians had set in motion a process that was still transforming Anglicanism,[2] and writing in the 1980s Geoffrey Rowell could ascribe to it an influence which affected not only the entire Anglican Communion but other traditions as well.[3] The Tractarian appeal to antiquity, therefore, cannot be ignored: it not only reveals what some Anglicans in the first half of the nineteenth century thought the Church of England was all about; it has also, for good or ill, found a permanent place within Anglican theology.

Background: The Need for an Authority other than Parliament

The widening of the franchise during the nineteenth century, which effectively allowed non-Anglicans to vote and sit in Parliament, meant

118

that the Church of England could no longer regard the House of Commons as its lay synod, at one mind with the clergy and dedicated to the maintenance of a national faith. In the light of this substantial shift in church-state relations, the Tractarians set out to find a basis for Anglican authority which was independent of Parliament. Their solution was to locate it in the teachings of the ancient Church. In reaction to Latitudinarianism (which in their eyes attached relatively little importance to questions of dogmatic truth, ecclesiastical organization and liturgical practice) and Protestantism (which they thought laid too much emphasis on the private individual's reading of Scripture), the Oxford Movement insisted that Anglicanism was the inheritor and defender of ancient catholic orthodoxy, and demanded obedience to its doctrines and practice. They summed up this position with the Vincentian Canon *quod ubique, quod semper, quod ab omnibus creditum est*.[4]

John Henry Newman's *Lectures on the Prophetical Office of the Church*[5] may be regarded as one of the best presentations of this Tractarian argument. It had considerable impact when it first appeared in 1836, and by 1890 R. W. Church was able to describe its thesis as the accepted Anglican view.[6] This praise was echoed forty years later when F. L. Cross described Newman's book as 'a magnificent apologia for what may be termed the Anglican ethos'.[7] This may be claiming more for the work than it deserves, but while it is debatable whether the *Prophetical Office* can be regarded as the final word on Anglicanism, it 'framed', in the words of Owen Chadwick, 'the most coherent, lucid and cogent argument for the Tractarian point of view'.[8] Newman's book, therefore, may act as a useful dialogue partner for a summary and critique of the Oxford Movement's appeal to antiquity.

The Prophetical Office of the Church (1836)

From the start Newman is concerned with developing an understanding of Church which is free of state control.[9] The Church should not base its self-understanding on its relationship with the state, but instead on its connections with antiquity. It is in its faithfulness to the teachings of the early Church that Anglicanism's true catholicity, its *Via Media* between Roman Catholicism and Protestantism, is located.[10] The tradition of the early Church, not Parliament, must become the guiding authority of the Church of England. Throughout his book Newman presents Anglicanism as the church which appeals to antiquity, is dedicated to the example of early church history and is obedient to its Creed.[11] It is here, in the ancient past, that the guiding doctrines of the true Church may be found.

Newman stresses the importance of this tradition in response to the claim that matters of religion are best left to the individual's private judgement. This, for him, has been the path of both Protestantism and Latitudinarianism, with the result that some of the Church's most central doctrines have fallen by the wayside. Protestantism, through its reliance on the doctrine of *sola scriptura* at the expense of tradition, has reduced the Christian faith to a matter of opinion.[12] Newman argues that on its own the Bible is confusing and open to contradictory and divisive interpretations, a malaise which he thinks afflicts all of Protestantism. To rely solely on the Bible as the source of truth, without the interpretive guidance of antiquity, is for him a self-destructive principle which allows every individual to form their own view of the meaning of Scripture.[13] While Anglicans may, in agreement with Protestants, consider Scripture a sufficient witness, they do not regard it as the sole guide to divine truths,[14] and rely 'on Antiquity to strengthen such intimations of doctrine as are but faintly, though really, given in Scripture'.[15] By appealing to antiquity, Anglicanism is in possession of a tradition which reveals the correct meaning of Scripture, free from the contradictions and divisions which afflict Protestantism.

Newman's real *bête noire*, however, is private judgement, in particular the version advanced by such groups as the Latitudinarians, who held that it is possible to grasp divine mysteries without the help of an external authority.[16] Newman argues forcefully against this view,[17] summing up his own thoughts in six points:

(1) That Scripture, Antiquity, and Catholicity cannot really contradict one another:

(2) That when the Moral Sense or the Reason of the individual seems to be on one side, and Scripture on the other, we must follow Scripture, except Scripture anywhere contained [sic] contradictions in terms, or prescribed undeniable crimes, which it never does:

(3) That when the sense of Scripture, as interpreted by the Reason of the individual, is contrary to the sense given to it by Catholic Antiquity, we ought to side with the latter:

(4) That when Antiquity runs counter to the present Church in important matters, we must follow Antiquity; when in unimportant matters, we must follow the present Church:

(5) That when the present Church speaks contrary to our private notions, and Antiquity is silent, or its decisions unknown to us, it is pious to sacrifice our own opinion to that of the Church:

(6) That if, in spite of our efforts to agree with the Church, we still differ from it, Antiquity being silent, we must avoid causing any disturbance, recollecting that the Church, and not individuals, 'has authority in controversies of faith'.[18]

The overall thrust is the subordination of individual reason to the authority of the Church, based on the Bible and the teachings of antiquity. While Newman is willing to admit the possibility of exceptions, it is clear that in religious matters he leaves almost no room for independent private judgement.[19]

Since Newman acknowledges the importance of tradition for correct scriptural interpretation, his criticism of Roman Catholicism is not as harsh as that reserved for Protestantism. While Rome has added corruptions, she still contains buried within her the faith of the early Church.[20] But in making this concession Newman is aware that he is in constant danger of drifting Romewards,[21] and it is important for him to show how the Anglican tradition is different from Roman Catholicism and more faithful to antiquity.[22] Later in the *Prophetical Office* it becomes clear that Newman's reverence for antiquity is based on his belief that the unity of the early Church gave it a greater infallibility than it has had in subsequent centuries. Since the ancient Church was one, its doctrines and teachings had not yet been damaged and distorted by divisive strife.[23] Newman seems to believe that historical inquiry alone will supply unambiguous factual knowledge of this almost infallible ancient tradition. Thus, in his eyes, he is building up Anglicanism on the sure foundation of historical facts, a fortress that cannot be assailed by more systematic and clever arguments.[24] The true Catholic Church protects these historical facts from distortion and enforces them among its members, if necessary through the power of excommunication.[25]

But what exactly is this permanent, unchangeable, ancient tradition that should be the basis of the true Catholic Church? Newman's answer is vague. In the first place, he is not even clear as to when antiquity ended. Newman is aware of this, but argues that an exact date is both unnecessary and unrealistic, because, first of all, the Church's impairment was not sudden but 'a question of degree and place', and, secondly, the historical documents suffer from imperfections which make it impossible to mark the exact point in history.[26] Thus he is prepared to identify the termination of antiquity at some point within a timespan covering over four hundred years: not much earlier than the Council of Sardia (347 CE) and not as late as the second Nicene or seventh General Council (787 CE).[27]

What is more striking, however, is that Newman traces the contents of ancient tradition right back to the first Apostles, arguing that from the beginning the Church possessed a 'Creed' which, at least implicitly, contained all the fundamental or essential doctrines. This 'Creed' is permanent and can neither be changed nor added to.[28] Thus the doctrines which are held by Anglicans, and which seem to have developed later in the early Church, must have been contained or anticipated in this 'Creed'.[29]

Newman is trying to ensure that such later definitions as the Nicene *homoousion* are not seen as additions but only interpretive clarifications of the static Apostolic witness.[30] Otherwise one would have to acknowledge the existence of doctrinal innovation within the early Church, and consequently admit that Rome is doing nothing new by making later additions to the faith, an admission which would threaten Newman's whole argument. Thus it is of paramount importance for him to demonstrate that the definitions of the ancient authoritative councils were clarifications, not innovations.[31] Newman draws a distinction between the content of the Creed, which has been the same from the very beginning, and its form, which has found varied expression in antiquity,[32] and is therefore able to argue that the Apostles' and Nicene Creeds are identical in content.[33]

This distinction between a fundamental 'Creed' and later clarifications is also necessary to defend the position of the Church of England, since it would be possible to claim that the Thirty-Nine Articles are innovations as well. Newman uses this distinction to separate 'articles of faith', which are the essential teachings of the Church and must be believed, from 'articles of religion', which only clarify the actual meaning of these essentials and thus are not mandatory for Church membership.[34] The former is part of what he calls the Church's 'Episcopal Tradition', while the latter belongs to its 'Prophetical Tradition'. The Episcopal Tradition ensures that the fundamental faith, the articles of faith, is handed down faithfully from generation to generation. The Prophetical Tradition, on the other hand, is there to expound properly this faith in changing historical circumstances; adherence to its teaching, while desirable, is not necessary.[35] Being articles of religion, the Thirty-Nine Articles belong to this Prophetical Tradition, and are therefore not additions to the original deposit of faith.

Newman's approach may seem plausible at first, but his artificial distinction between Episcopal and Prophetical Tradition causes serious methodological difficulties. The success of his argument is dependent on his ability to deliver an adequate description of the doctrines contained within this original 'Creed' defended by the Episcopal Tradition. Unfortunately, in spite of claims to the contrary,[36] he fails to do so, and it remains unclear how in practice the Episcopal Tradition is to be differentiated from the Prophetical. Indeed, although he tries to play down its significance, Newman himself is forced to admit that a distinct line between the two cannot be drawn.[37]

This admission undermines his whole argument. Newman is intent on basing Anglicanism's authority on the teachings of antiquity, and he goes to great lengths to insist that this ancient tradition, this fundamental 'Creed', is obeyed at all times. But his failure to give an adequate summary of the contents of this 'Creed' means that in the end he is unable to define orthodoxy. Indeed, he appears not to realize that his distinction between 'articles of faith' and 'articles of religion' threatens to undermine the authority of even the most cherished credal statements of the early Church. For example, by arguing that the Nicene Creed did not add anything to the original 'Creed', but instead only clarified what was already given, Newman is actually describing this Creed in the same way as he does the Thirty-Nine Articles, as an article of religion. In practice this would mean that adherence to the Nicene Creed should not be necessary for Church membership. But how, then, is the expulsion of the Arians from the ancient Church to be justified, since it was based on the definitions of this very creed? Following the logic of Newman's own argument, the answer would seem to be that it cannot be justified. By making the distinction between Episcopal and Prophetical Tradition, Newman sets up a false dichotomy which ensures that the very orthodoxy he is so keen to protect disappears in methodological confusion.[38]

Newman's attempt to reconcile his reliance on a continuing ancient tradition with his idea of a permanent, unalterable 'Creed', leads him into a position where it becomes impossible to elaborate the orthodoxy which is so dear to him. But even if he could supply an adequate description of this 'Creed', it is questionable whether his view of Anglicanism is anything other than partial. He appears to ignore the fact that the Church of England's identity was also shaped by the thoughts and practices of the Reformation.

Newman has no time for individuals reading the Bible on their own authority, and insists that they must bow to the traditions of the Church in order to acquire the proper interpretation. Indeed, he goes so far as to reject a basic Reformation principle by arguing that it is tradition, not Scripture that brings people to faith.[39] The Church, as a bearer and witness to this ancient tradition, is the binding authority for every individual. While Newman is prepared to grant at least the possibility of dissent,[40] the general thrust of his argument is built on the presupposition that the individual must bow to the teachings of the Church. If, in all good conscience, they cannot do this, they are to remain silent in order not to cause unnecessary disturbance.[41] In the end almost all is subordinate to tradition.

Anglicanism, however, does not necessarily deny the Protestant idea that individual judgement may influence biblical interpretation. Article VI of the Thirty-Nine Articles is at best ambiguous on this matter, for while it states that only those teachings need be believed which may be verified in Scripture, it does not say *who* actually does this verifying.[42] It is, therefore, possible to read this article as permitting individual interpretation of the Bible. For example, in his exposition of this article in 1699 Bishop Gilbert Burnet presents a very negative view of tradition. Tradition was what sects used to give their heresies credibility: Jews appealed to it in their disagreements with Jesus, and the Gnostics and Valentinians used it in their own defence.[43] For Burnet 'oral tradition appears, both from the nature of man, and the experience of former times, to be an incompetent conveyor of truth', and he insists that 'whatsoever appears to be clearly the sense of any place of scripture, is an object of faith...'.[44] Burnet acknowledges that Scripture can be confusing, but instead of turning to tradition for the proper interpretation, he uses this fact to argue that people must read the Bible carefully and piously without 'submitting to the dictates of others'.[45] For Burnet Article VI clearly states the importance of the individual's reading of Scripture free from the dictates of tradition, and his exposition is a good example of how, at least in part, the Reformation principle of *sola scriptura* influenced Anglican thought.[46] Newman's heavy stress on tradition, therefore, seems deliberately to avoid the ambiguity of Article VI. Newman appears to be aware of this,[47] for he spends the three penultimate chapters of the *Prophetical Office* trying to reconcile his argument with Article VI.

Reading Article VI in conjunction with Article XX,[48] Newman attempts to demonstrate that the former is not directed at the individual but at the Church; it tells the Church what she is permitted to teach.[49] Newman ascribes to Scripture only a negative function; it tells the Church when its tradition is in error. This Newman describes as Anglicanism's 'double rule':[50] 'Scripture is interpreted by Tradition, Tradition is verified by Scripture'.[51]

This, however, raises the question of who does the actual verifying. Newman's own argument seems to suggest that it is the Church itself. The individual may disagree only in areas where the Church does not claim authority.[52] But the Church, as the guardian of ancient tradition, definitely claims authority in matters of scriptural interpretation, which in practice means that she is in full control of a source that could criticize her. Only if the individual were given the right to use Scripture to disagree with tradition would Newman's understanding of the 'double rule' work, but his whole argument ensures that the individual will never have this kind of independence. In short, in spite of his protestations to the contrary, Newman is unable to reconcile Article VI, which at least allows for the possibility of individual judgement, with his understanding of Anglicanism, which does not. In practice, true authority continues to lie in tradition, and not in Scripture as interpreted by the individual believer.

One of the main problems with Newman's entire reconstruction of Anglicanism is its ambiguity on matters of authority. Newman may stress that tradition appeals to antiquity and is verified by Scripture, but it is unclear where it is actually located and maintained. At first glance this ambiguity is not apparent, since it would seem that authority lies with the bishop. Newman himself was quite specific in seeing the bishop as the protector and transmitter of the Episcopal Tradition.[53] Reflecting on his Anglican years in *Apologia Pro Vita Sua* (1864), Newman admits that he saw his bishop as the final authority: '[W]hat to me was *jure divino* was the voice of my Bishop in his own person. My own Bishop was my Pope; I knew no other; the successor of the Apostles, the Vicar of Christ'.[54] Indeed, during his participation in the Oxford Movement Newman was intent on developing the latent powers of the episcopate so that it could function as the centre and emblem of Christian unity and as the guardian of sound doctrine.[55] In practice, however, both the Tractarians in general and Newman in particular were quite prepared to disobey their bishop when they disagreed. Thus, for instance, the moderate High Church prelate Samuel Wilberforce had problems with the obstreperous Edward Pusey, and the Oxford tracts, especially Newman's Tract 90, received the episcopal bench's united disapproval.[56] This ambiguity in the Tractarians' obedience towards their bishops leads S. W. Sykes and S. W. Gilley to accuse them of double standards: 'You exalted your bishop as an angel, but if the angel called you to order you defied him'.[57]

Defiance became possible because the Tractarian appeal to antiquity contained within it a subtle, but significant, shift in the basis of authority. As Newman's *Prophetical Office* shows, they wanted to return to the teachings of the undivided early Church, and consequently emphasized the need to read early church history and the early Fathers. What the Tractarians failed to appreciate was that this emphasis on antiquity effectively removed authority from the bishop and placed it in the hands of the church historian. Thus, when a bishop made pronouncements which, in Tractarian eyes, went contrary to the teachings of antiquity, they felt themselves theoretically justified as early church historians (if not as priests) to resist him in the name of true orthodoxy.

This ambivalence in their obedience towards the episcopate suggests that private judgement, that bane which Newman was so keen to eradicate, crept into their own understanding of Anglicanism through the back door of historical inquiry. Newman may have denied individuals the right to determine the sense of Scripture, but he did believe that individuals could agree on the content of ancient church history if they took the time to read it objectively.[58] Unfortunately, the individual's private judgment, shaped by personal, historical, geographical and sociological factors, also impinges on the reading of church history, and one person's orthodox interpretation may be another's heresy. Thus the Tractarians' inadequate appreciation of the subjectivity of historical inquiry led them to regard their own interpretations as accurate and those of their opponents as contrary to 'fact'. On this basis defiance of the bishop became possible.

Conclusion

This excursion into the theology of the Anglican Newman demonstrates how the appeal to antiquity is, in the end, only of limited value, since it remains virtually impossible to reach an acceptable consensus on how the past is to be approached and interpreted. Also, by making an unrealistic distinction between the original, permanent deposit of faith, and its varied expressions in changing historical circumstances, the entire argument sets up a false dichotomy between content and form which leaves it unclear why the teachings of antiquity, themselves expressed within a particular historical situation, should be more authoritative than others. The issue of authority is also not addressed adequately. Who in fact determines the authentic tradition, safeguards it, and re-expresses it in the contemporary setting? The historian, the bishop, or both of them? Does Anglicanism even grant them the power to do so? And, last but not least, does not the appeal to antiquity ignore the fact that Anglicanism was also influenced heavily by the ideas of the Reformation? The problems raised by these questions are not dealt with, and in the end the 'antiquity' hypothesis remains just that, a hypothesis, without adequate practical application.

Notes

1. The following is indebted to Stephen Thomas's observations in his *Newman and Heresy. The Anglican Years* (Cambridge University Press, Cambridge, 1991).

2. Frank Leslie Cross, *John Henry Newman* (Philip Allan, Glasgow, 1933), p. 6.
3. Geoffrey Rowell, *The Vision Glorious. Themes and Personalities of the Catholic Revival in Anglicanism* (Oxford University Press, Oxford, 1983), pp. v, 20, 251.
4. Owen Chadwick, *From Bossuet to Newman* (2nd edn.; Cambridge University Press, London, 1987), p. 88. cf. David L. Edwards, *Christian England* (Collins, London, 1984), Vol.2: p. 181.
5. John Henry Newman, *The Via Media of the Anglican Church* (ed. and intr. H. D. Weidner; Clarendon Press, Oxford, 1990), pp. 11-12. Weidner's edition is based on the 1889 edition of Newman's work, and contains an appendix of the variant readings of the 1836 and 1837 editions. In the margins he has maintained the 1889 pagination in order to facilitate reference to the uniform edition of the collected works. For the same reasons I refer to the page numbers in the margins.
6. R. W. Church, *The Oxford Movement: Twelve Years 1833-1845* (Macmillan, London, 1891), p. 186.
7. Cross, op. cit., p. 70.
8. Chadwick, op. cit., p. 87.
9. Newman, *Via Media of the Anglican Church*, op. cit., pp. 11-12.
10. ibid., p. 7.
11. ibid., p, 167. This same appeal to read early church history may already be found in Newman's Tract 40 of 1834.
12. Newman, *Via Media of the Anglican Church*, op. cit., p. 27.
13. ibid., pp. 26-27.
14. ibid., p. 28. The heading of Article VI of the Thirty-Nine Articles speaks 'Of the Sufficiency of the holy Scriptures for Salvation'. The Hanson brothers consider this word 'sufficiency' to be 'a good Anglican word', since it means that the biblical material is sufficient for its readers to understand about their salvation, while at the same time suggesting that the Bible cannot be expected 'to be a magic book to answer all questions, or a carefully contrived and concerted system of omnicompetent theology . . .' A. T. & R. P. C. Hanson, *Reasonable Belief. A Survey of the Christian Faith* (Oxford University Press, Oxford, 1981), p. 44.
15. Newman, *Via Media of the Anglican Church*, op. cit., p. 29.
16. ibid., p. 145.
17. ibid., pp. 129-131.
18. ibid., pp. 134-135. The quotation is from article XX of the Thirty-Nine Articles.
19. cf. ibid., p. 214. Nevertheless, Newman made great claims for the individual conscience, establishing a fundamental identity between it and the voice of God. It would be important for future Newman studies to see how far he was able to reconcile this view with his idea of the Church's supreme authority. See S. A. Grave, *Conscience in Newman's Thought* (Clarendon Press, Oxford, 1989).
20. Newman, *Via Media of the Anglican Church*, op. cit., p. 40.
21. Thomas, op. cit., p. 4.

22. 'We deny that his [i. e. the Roman Catholic's] doctrines are in Antiquity any more than they are in the Bible; and we maintain that his professed Tradition is not really such, that it is a Tradition of men, that it is not continuous, that it stops short of the Apostles, that the history of its introduction is known. On both accounts then his doctrines are innovations; because they run counter to the doctrine of Antiquity, and because they rest upon what is historically an upstart Tradition.' Newman, *Via Media of the Anglican Church*, op. cit., pp. 37-38.

23. ibid., pp. 199-203.

24. ibid., p. 79.

25. ibid., p. 189; cf. p. 140.

26. ibid., p. 204.

27. ibid., p. 207.

28. ibid., pp. 217-218, 224, 228-229.

29. 'Even granting there were articles of faith which as yet lay, amid the general traditionary teaching, undefined and unrecognized in public formularies, such as the Divinity of the Holy Ghost, is it not plain that still they must have been implied and virtually contained in the Creed . . . ?' ibid., p. 222.

30. ibid., p. 225.

31. '[I]s there no difference between adding a word and adding a doctrine, between explaining what is in the Creed and inserting what was not in it? Surely it was not inconsistent with the reverence due to it, for the Church Catholic, after careful deliberation, to clear up any ambiguity which, as time went on, might be found to exist in its wording. The words of the [Nicene] Creed were not inspired; they were only valuable in expressing a certain sense, and if they were found deficient in expressing that sense, there was as little interference with things sacred, as little real change, in correcting or supplying what was needful, as in completing the lines of a chart by the original. The original was the one universally received Faith, which was in the minds and mouths of all Christians without variation or ambiguity.' ibid., pp. 225-226.

32. ibid., p. 226. Aidan Nichols shows how this attempt to avoid Rome was to prove self-contradictory, and lead Newman to the idea of the development of doctrine. Aidan Nichols, *From Newman to Congar. The Idea of Doctrinal Development from the Victorians to the Second Vatican Council* (T & T Clark, Edinburgh, 1990), pp. 27-37.

33. Newman, *Via Media of the Anglican Church*, op. cit., p. 227.

34. ibid., p. 234.

35. ibid., pp. 249-251.

36. ibid., p. 218; cf. p. 239.

37. ibid., p. 254.

38. Stephen Thomas explores in considerable detail how this very problem affected most of the work of the Anglican Newman. He remarks: 'His uncertainty about the exact content of the fundamentals and their relation to Antiquity is so persistent as to imply a chronic inability to declare what orthodoxy is.' Thomas, op. cit., p. 194.

39. 'It is not true in fact, and never will be, that the mass of serious Christians derive their faith for themselves from the Scriptures. No; they derive it from Tradition, whether true or corrupt; and they are intended by Divine Providence to derive it from the true, viz., that which the Church Catholic has ever furnished...' Newman, *Via Media of the Anglican Church*, op. cit., p. 244.
40. ibid., p. 268.
41. ibid., pp. 134-135.
42. Article VI says in part: 'Holy Scripture containeth all things necessary to salvation: so that whatsoever is not read therein, nor may be proved thereby, is not to be required of any man, that it should be believed as an article of the Faith, or be thought requisite or necessary to salvation.'
43. Gilbert Burnet, *An Exposition of the Thirty-Nine Articles of the Church of England* (rev. and corrected Rev. James R. Page; Scott, Webster, and Geary, London, 1837), pp. 94-96.
44. ibid., p. 97.
45. ibid., pp. 98-99.
46. This influence is apparent in the Preface to the 1549 Prayer Book which states 'that all the whole Bible . . . should be read over once every year; intending thereby, that the Clergy, and especially such as were Ministers in the Congregation, should (by often reading and meditating in God's Word) be stirred up to godliness themselves, and be more able to exhort others by wholesome doctrine, and to confute them that were Adversaries to the Truth; and further, that the people (by daily hearing of holy Scripture read in the Church) might continually profit more and more in the knowledge of God, and be the more inflamed with the love of his true Religion.' Quoted from the Church of Ireland *Book of Common Prayer* (APCK, Dublin, 1960), p. xi. See also G. J. Cuming, *A History of Anglican Liturgy* (2nd. ed.; Macmillan, London, 1982), pp. 45-47. More recently Stephen Sykes, in reference to Article VI, has acknowledged that independent individual interpretation of the Bible is an integral part of Anglicanism: 'The possession by ordinary clergy and by the laity of the means of judgement in matters relating to the integrity of the faith and to the proper preaching of the gospel is crucial for the Anglican understanding of authority. It means that whatever machinery a church may devise for making decisions, and with whatever spiritual powers this machinery may adorn itself, at the end of the day the people of God have the means of judging, independently if need be, whether or not the truth is being upheld.' Stephen Sykes, *The Integrity of Anglicanism* (Mowbray, London, Oxford, 1978), pp. 90-91.
47. Newman, *Via Media of the Anglican Church*, op. cit., p. 266.
48. Article XX reads: 'The Church hath power to decree Rites or Ceremonies, and authority in Controversies of Faith: And yet it is not lawful for the Church to ordain any thing that is contrary to God's Word written, neither may it so expound one place of Scripture, that it be repugnant to another. Wherefore, although the Church be a witness and a keeper of holy Writ, yet, as it ought not to decree any thing against

the same, so besides the same ought not to enforce any thing to be
believed for necessity of Salvation.'

49. 'The sole question, I say, in the Articles *is how the Church is to teach*.
Thus, in the sixth it is said, that nothing but what is contained in
Scripture, or may be proved by it, is to be *"required* of any man that it
should be believed as an article of faith.*"* And the 20th still more clearly:
*"*It is not lawful *for the Church to ordain* anything that is contrary to
God's word written, neither may *it so expound* one place of Scripture
that it be repugnant to another. Wherefore, although the *Church* be
witness and a keeper of Holy Writ, yet as it ought not to *decree* anything
against the same, so besides the same ought it not to *enforce* anything
to be believed for necessity of salvation.*"* It does not say what individuals may do, but what the Church may not do.' Newman, *Via Media of
the Anglican Church*, op. cit., pp. 271-272.

50. ibid., p. 273.

51. ibid., p. 274.

52. ibid., pp. 268, 273.

53. ibid., p. 249.

54. John Henry Newman, *Apologia Pro Vita Sua* (The Catholic Book Club,
London, 1946), p. 34.

55. Ian Ker, *John Henry Newman. A Biography* (Oxford University Press,
Oxford, New York, 1988), p. 115.

56. Stephen Sykes & S. W. Gilley, '"No Bishop, No Church!"' in Geoffrey
Rowell, ed., *Tradition Renewed. The Oxford Movement Conference
Papers* (Darton, Longman and Todd, London, 1986), p. 131.

57. ibid. See also p. 132.

58. Newman, *Via Media of the Anglican Church*, op. cit., p. 109.

The Rise of Liberal Catholic Pastoral Theology 1883–1912

Peter Davie

I

When Michael Ramsey set out to survey Anglican theology 'from Gore to Temple' he began by noting that 'Anglican theology has through the years been written chiefly in universities, in vicarages and (alas, with diminishing frequency) in episcopal residences'. [1] One branch of Anglican theology, which Ramsey did not touch upon, has rarely been written in universities. Most pastoral theology has been composed in vicarages and episcopal residences.

In 1907 King's College London broke with this tradition when it appointed C. F. Rogers (1866–1949) to a new lectureship in pastoral theology. In his lectures Rogers argued for a radical change in the discipline. The old pastoral handbooks were too amateur to be adequate guides to pastoral care in the twentieth century. Parsons should follow the lead of teachers, doctors and social workers; they should base pastoral care upon an empirically-based discipline comparable to medicine, educational theory or social administration. [2] Before taking up his post at King's College, Rogers had served as an assistant curate in several London parishes. He had also acquired an expertise in social administration as a lecturer at the first college for social workers recently established by the Charity Organisation Society. [3] In 1905 he wrote about the confusion that he believed existed in many priests' minds about what they should be doing, and about the poor standards of clerical work which put off promising young men from entry into the ministry. [4] Rogers' answer to these problems was to promote a new empirical discipline – 'a scientific treatment of Pastoral Theology' – based upon 'induction as the

131

ordinary method of science begun by Bacon and established by Darwin'.[5]

When Rogers surveyed the literature of traditional pastoral theology he found it wanting. An impressive Roman Catholic pastoral tradition was based upon outmoded methods. Protestant practical theology was more promising but rested upon defective ideas about the Church and ministry, and was largely restricted to preaching. Anglicans retained vital aspects of Catholic tradition and a wider view of pastoral care in the Book of Common Prayer, but their pastoral theology too remained amateur and unsystematic. Even the classic work of Anglican pastoral theology, George Herbert's *The Country Parson*, represented no more than the amateur ideal of a Christian gentleman at work in his parish. The pastoral handbooks of the eighteenth and nineteenth centuries had merely followed Herbert and achieved no real advance on his ideas.[6]

Rogers' low estimate of Anglican pastoral theology appears to have been shared by subsequent theologians and church historians. While the literary merits of *The Country Parson* have been widely admired, and pastoral handbooks have been referred to by historians, there has been no sustained discussion of the history of pastoral theology as a theological discipline.

The argument of this essay is that, like many innovators, Rogers exaggerated the defects of his predecessors, and that an examination of the development of Liberal Catholic pastoral theology in the Church of England from 1883 to 1912 shows that Anglican pastoral theology is of greater interest and significance than has been hitherto recognised. Further, it will be argued, a tradition of pastoral theology was established which continues to be of significance for Anglicans today.

II

The term 'pastoral theology' is used in several ways: to describe the adaptation of theology and doctrine to pastoral use; or to describe attempts to think about pastoral care theologically. Our present interest is in pastoral theology in the latter sense. 'Pastoral care' is also a term that is used in different ways: in a narrow sense to describe one aspect of a minister's work – that of counselling and caring for individuals; or more traditionally to describe the whole of a pastor's work in caring for his flock. In Anglican tradition 'pastoral care' has been used in a broad sense to cover preaching, teaching, leading worship, administering sacraments, as well as offering moral and spiritual counsel to individuals.[7]

The chief source of Anglican pastoral theology is the Book of

Common Prayer. The Prayer Book ordination services for deacons and priests outline the life and work of the Anglican pastor. He is set apart as a man of God to devote his life to prayer and study. He is to offer pastoral care to the flock committed to his charge, by feeding them with God's gracious word in preaching and teaching, and in the administration of the sacraments. He leads his flock in worship. He sanctifies each significant stage in his people's progress from birth to death: he baptizes them, prepares them for confirmation, marries them and buries them. He offers individual moral and spiritual guidance, together with the opportunity for confession and absolution.

This Prayer Book pattern of pastoral care was enlarged upon and adapted to changing circumstances in the pastoral handbooks of the seventeenth and eighteenth centuries. In the early Victorian period the religious revival brought about by Evangelicalism and the Oxford Movement, together with the administrative reforms of the 1830s, issued in a pastoral revival in the parishes of the Church of England. New pastoral handbooks were written to guide a new and more earnest generation of clergymen in their work in the light of Evangelical or Tractarian theological principles.

One of the most notable of these early Victorian pastoral handbooks was Edward Monro's *Parochial Work* (1850). Monro (1815–1866) was a Tractarian who believed that the Book of Common Prayer was the ideal basis for a revival of pastoral care along High Church lines. John Keble described his book as 'our modern Country Parson' and praised it for basing its pastoral system upon the sacraments. Such a system, Keble argued, struck far deeper roots in the souls of the people than the Evangelical system, which merely stirred up short-lived emotions through an over-emphasis upon preaching.[8]

Monro believed that the chief problem in most rural parishes was that the mass of poor people had little idea of Anglican faith and practice. The blame for this should not be laid at their doors but at those of the generations of clergy who had been content to live as country gentlemen and to neglect their pastoral obligations. The clergy must abandon their lives of ease and serve the poor by offering them all the benefits of the Prayer Book pastoral system.[9]

The foundation of this pastoral system was the devout administration of baptism, with parents and godparents properly instructed that baptism is not a mere naming ceremony, but the very means of regeneration and the true beginning of the Christian life.[10] The revival of the proper administration of baptism should be accompanied by a like revival of the regular and devout celebration of the Holy Communion each Sunday and Holy Day as prescribed in the rubrics of the Prayer Book. If the sacraments were the jewels in the crown of parish worship, their setting was the daily and public recitation of Morning and Evening Prayer. The poor had to be encouraged and enabled to attend by priests willing to get up early and turn out late to lead worship at times convenient to all. Attendance at the daily offices would divert the poor from public houses and radical meetings, and they would acquire a 'devout habit of mind' through the regular offering of penitence and praise.[11]

Nevertheless there was little chance of inducing the poor to attend worship or to participate in the sacraments with devotion without first arousing in them a sense of spiritual need. Although Monro did not regard preaching as a 'direct channel' of grace like the sacraments, he did believe that it was vital to awakening a sense of need for a personal religious faith. In addition to preaching there were two other main ways of achieving this: the spiritual guidance of adults and the catechetical instruction of children.

The pastoral guidance of individuals was a 'foremost work' of the conscientious parson. Apart from discharging their duty to visit the sick the clergy should avoid the aimless social chatter of home visits. Parishioners should be encouraged instead to attend regularly at the parsonage where it was easier to concentrate upon moral and spiritual guidance. In an average rural parish it should be possible to see each parishioner often enough to make systematic guidance feasible.[12] Important as this work was, however, it was doubtful if it could be wholly fruitful. Most adults were fixed in their habits. Children were more open and pliable. The Prayer Book pattern for nurturing the young was to teach them the catechism, which should be done in school on weekdays as well as in church on Sundays.[13]

Monro presents a coherent and systematic approach to the adaptation of the Prayer Book pattern of pastoral care to meet the needs of the mid-nineteenth century rural parish. His pastoral theology is based upon the Anglo-Catholic emphasis upon sacramental mediation as the chief means of promoting communion with God, with preaching and teaching as vital ancillaries. In the second half of the nineteenth century the High Church movement became increasingly powerful in the parishes, and many pastoral handbooks were based upon a similar interpretation of the Anglican pastoral system. There were, however, major limitations to Monro's approach which soon became apparent to later pastoral theologians.

III

In 1850 Edward Monro briefly noted the problems of the town parish, but devoted his attentions to the village parish he knew best. Fourteen years later John Henry Blunt insisted that the clergy must recognise that England was now a 'land of manufacturing and commercial towns, as well of agricultural villages'. In the towns advances in secular education and knowledge had led to a new air of questioning and to criticism of ancient truths. Men and women were turning away from the Church to the halfway house of Dissent, and from thence to Secularism. Blunt's widely used pastoral handbook systematically adapted the High Church pastoral system to the needs of the urban parish, but maintained the conservative theological outlook of Monro and the Tractarians.[14]

By the early 1880s, however, it was accepted on all sides that the major pastoral problems of the urban parish – religious indifference, poverty and the growth of religious doubt in all classes – required a new approach to pastoral theology and methods of pastoral work. William Walsham How (1823–1897) dwelt on these problems and their solution in 1883 in the first series of what became annual Lent lectures in pastoral theology at Cambridge.

Walsham How went up to Oxford in 1841, where he came under the Tractarian influences which led him to seek ordination. In later life he remained loyal to the movement's early ideals although he rejected Ritualism. During a long period as a country parson he became widely known as the author of popular hymns and devotional manuals. In 1879 he was made Bishop of Bedford, a suffragan bishop of St Albans, in charge (at that time) of the vast working-class area of East London.[15] In his Cambridge lectures on 'pastoral work' he declared that the pastoral problems that had preoccupied the previous generation of parsons – Dissent, Roman Catholicism, biblical inspiration – had now to take second place to the problems of mass religious indifference, and the widespread questioning of the fundamentals of religious faith itself. Many Churchmen said the cause of unbelief was immoral lives, but How dismissed this as 'simply a libel'. The chief cause of modern unbelief was intellectual doubt, which had to be taken seriously. While there were some who shouted for Bradlaugh[16] thoughtlessly and others who were too easily content 'to live without God', most doubters were 'very honest minded, thoughtful and truth seeking'. The current 'sifting, testing and analysing' of religious belief should be welcomed as part of the 'great truth seeking spirit of the age'. The Christian faith could emerge from this period of testing purified and strengthened, but if it was to do so the clergy had to face the problems honestly, and show themselves able to state the case for Christianity clearly and intelligently.[17]

Like Monro a generation before, How believed that in the long run the most hopeful pastoral strategy was to teach Christian faith and practice to the young. But where Monro was suspicious of teachers and their methods, How believed the clergy should be prepared to learn from them. Yet he insisted that education was more than mere secular instruction; that the purpose of school was to 'lead souls to God'; and that the clergy should appeal to hearts and consciences as well as to intellects. Nevertheless he believed that children should be taught the rudiments of biblical criticism; that the 'phenomenal language of the Bible was never meant to reveal the secrets of physics'; and that 'a blind adhesion to the once popular and still largely cherished idea of rigid verbal inspiration' was not required of modern believers. Older pupils should also be taught some basic philosophical theology, and shown that the theory of evolution did not refute the argument from design, as was widely supposed, but rather strengthened it. Children should be taught 'conceptions of God' that would stand them in good stead against the onset of doubt in later life.[18]

William Walsham How belonged to a new and more liberal generation of High Church pastoral theologians. While remaining loyal to the basic tenets of early Tractarianism, he wished to combine High Church ideals with a heartfelt devotion akin to that of Evangelicalism, together with an open-minded acceptance of biblical criticism and evolutionary science. With regard to pastoral methods he was willing to learn from teachers and other secular professions. How's theological outlook was an early expression of what came to be known as 'Liberal Catholicism'.

IV

At the end of the 1880s the most famous book of Liberal Catholic theology – *Lux Mundi* – made its appearance. Among a number of notable pastoral theologians of this school of thought the most distinguished was Cosmo Gordon Lang (1860–1942), a future Archbishop of Canterbury. As a student at Balliol, Lang's theological sympathies lay less with its famous Broad Church Master, Benjamin Jowett, than with the rising young Anglo-Catholic leader Charles Gore, the editor of *Lux Mundi*. Lang wished to 'stand with those who have incorporated many of the best elements of the High Church ideal with the teaching of men like Maurice and Kingsley'. He wanted to combine the 'firm sacramental teaching which was the kernel of the Oxford Movement, with the candour, freedom and breadth of view which marked Maurice and Kingsley and Robertson of Brighton'.[19]

Ordained deacon in 1890 he rapidly ran through a broad range of parish experiences before being made Bishop of Stepney in 1901: a brief curacy at Leeds Parish Church, a spell in Oxford, and, finally, the incumbency of the huge parish of Portsea with its team of curates serving a large number of daughter churches. In 1904 he brought liberal Catholic theology and pastoral experience to bear upon 'the opportunities of the Church of England' in six pastoral theology lectures at Cambridge.

He told his students that the Church faced two main evils: 'the dissolution of definite belief and practice'; and the religious indifference of the masses. The causes and cures of these twin evils should be the key themes of a modern pastoral theology.[20]

In discussing the causes of working class religious indifference he drew upon the recent investigations by social scientists into popular beliefs. Charles Booth's survey of the East End of London had highlighted the extent of working class alienation from religious observance. Mudie-Smith's *Religious Life of London* had confirmed that only one-fifth of all Londoners attended any place of worship regularly on Sundays, and that barely one in a hundred of working class men in the East End ever appeared in a church or chapel on a Sunday.[21]

Lang traced the roots of this religious apathy to the failure of parents to teach their children prayers or Bible stories, or to take them to church. Most working class parents were too deadened and demoralised by conditions at work and at home to spare any thought for God or religion. They were not so much opposed to religion as indifferent to matters remote from their daily needs and concerns.

The dissolution of definite Christian beliefs and practices had spread to all classes, and was the result of a variety of causes. Universal elementary education had produced a generation able to read and write but ill-equipped to assess what they read in popular newspapers and magazines. As a consequence many were easily swayed by the specious arguments of anti-religious propaganda that science disproved religion or that the Bible had been shown to be fiction. These secularist ideas merely reinforced and further entrenched the working class belief in 'a diffused Christianity', which sat loose to doctrine and sacrament and identified Christianity with little more than moral ideals.[22]

Like Walsham How, Lang believed it was yet possible for the parochial clergy to turn back the tide of indifference and unbelief. If they were to do so they must become more effective teachers of the faith, willing to learn from new advances in the theory and practice of education. They must learn to teach authoritatively without being authoritarian; to present Christian truths in a variety of ways suited to various audiences; to avoid abstractions and to relate their message to concrete human concerns. At the same time they must keep up with advances in theology so as to be able to deal with questions about science and biblical criticism in ways that would convince sceptical listeners.[23]

Like other Liberal Catholics, Lang wanted the clergy to reject the negative aspects of Evangelicalism and the older forms of Anglo-Catholicism, as he saw them, and to stress instead the human and social significance of the Word made flesh. They should stress that Jesus Christ not only saves men and women from sin but also 'vindicates true humanity in the Incarnation'. The Church should be shown to be a 'living, many-functional brotherhood', concerned about charity, brotherliness and social service. The 'best sort of working man' would be attracted to a church community which was close to early Christian patterns of fellowship.[24]

V

Our brief sketch of Victorian and Edwardian Anglican pastoral theology is no more than an outline, yet it is possible to discern some main lines of development. Monro represents the conservatism of the post-Tractarian period rooted in the rural pastoral tradition that looked back to George Herbert and the Book of Common Prayer, which stressed the centrality of priestly-sacramental mediation, and sought to create a total Church community in each parish.

A more liberal interpretation of Anglican Catholicism emerged in the pastoral writings of William Walsham How and Cosmo Gordon Lang. They took the re-establishment of sacramental worship in Anglican parishes for granted and concentrated upon the pressing needs of the urban parish – particularly working class alienation and the growth of religious doubt. Both stressed the need for the parson to become a more adequate teacher of the faith and pressed the claims of modern theology and educational theory as aids in doing so.

Enough has been said to call into question C.F. Rogers' judgement, that the Anglican tradition of pastoral theology was inadequate and amateurish in approach. In their pastoral writings Edward Monro, William Walsham How and Cosmo Gordon Lang made systematic attempts to bring theology to bear upon the pastoral problems of the day. The Liberal Catholics, Lang in particular, also made use of current findings in the social sciences and educational theory, as well as in biblical criticism and other branches of theology.

Rogers did advance a step further than his predecessors. He insisted on the need for a full investigation of pastoral theological method – a topic hitherto ignored or taken for granted by most previous pastoral writers. One who was not wholly guilty of this neglect was John

Pilkington Norris (1823–1891), a High Church Archdeacon of Bristol. In his opening lecture of the 1884 series of pastoral theology lectures at Cambridge he considered pastoral theological method in the light of the ideas of Johann Michael Sailer (1751–1839), the pioneer of German Catholic pastoral theology. He followed Sailer in defining pastoral theology as 'theology in its application to the care of souls'. Its method was to be deductive: guidelines for pastoral practice were to be deduced from the axioms of biblical and dogmatic theology. Norris made explicit the approach most traditional pastoral theologians implicitly followed, usually without much reflection.[25] In 1903 James Michael Wilson (1836–1931), the Broad Church Archdeacon of Manchester, devoted all six of his Cambridge pastoral theology lectures to an attempt to recast the discipline as an empirical science based upon the inductive method. Pastoral theology like all branches of theology must reflect upon human religious experience both as recorded in the Bible (above all in the life of Jesus) and in contemporary life. The test of the worth of the interpretations and formulations made by theologians should be practical: how far they help lift 'man nearer God'.[26]

When Rogers discussed pastoral theology in 1912 he too concentrated upon the aims and methods of the discipline. In his view theology is the science of our relationship to God 'as it presents itself to reason'. Pastoral theology is the study of the pastoral ministrations of the clergy in their attempts to help their parishioners to enter into communion with God. Rogers believed that the clergy were failing in that task because they were following outdated approaches. In teaching children, for example, they relied upon rote learning and failed to utilize empirically based findings about the best ways to present lessons and to help children learn.[27]

Rogers argued with all the enthusiasm of a convert who believed that with him Anglican pastoral theology was beginning all over again. The evidence of this essay is that the Liberal Catholic approaches of William Walsham How and Cosmo Gordon Lang already signified a major shift in pastoral theological thought. The traditionalism of the older post-Tractarian tradition was significantly modified by a greater openness to modern findings in a variety of fields – biblical criticism, educational theory and so on. Rogers wrote from within this tradition. As an academic he had more time than most of his predecessors to reflect upon questions of method systematically, but he was working from within a tradition that they had already established.

The life and work of the parson is one of the most notable features of Anglican history, yet the history of clerical attempts to reflect upon their task has been largely neglected. The aim of this essay has been to demonstrate, from a small specimen of that history, that Anglican pastoral theology is worthy of study. Further, the Liberal Catholic tradition of pastoral theology, which developed out of the earlier Tractarian tradition in the late Victorian and Edwardian periods, remains a living force. The writings of Michael Ramsey and Martin Thornton demonstrate that Liberal Catholic pastoral theology has yet much to contribute to the future of Anglicanism[28].

Notes

1. A.M. Ramsey, *From Gore to Temple: The Development of Anglican theology between Lux Mundi and the Second World War 1889-1939* (Longmans, London, 1961), p.1.
2. C.F. Rogers, *An Introduction to the Study of Pastoral Theology* (Clarendon Press, Oxford, 1912).
3. M.J. Smith, *Professional Educational for Social Work in Britain: An Historical Account* (Allen and Unwin, London, 1965), p.43.
4. C.F. Rogers, *Principles of Pastoral Work: An Essay in Pastoral Theology* (London, 1905), p.viii.
5. Rogers (1912), op.cit., p.23.
6. ibid., p.52.
7. See O.C. Edwards, 'Anglican Pastoral Tradition', S. Sykes and J. Booty, eds. *The Study of Anglicanism* (SPCK, London, 1989), p.338.
8. J. Keble, *Occasional Papers and Reviews* (Parker, Oxford, 1877), p.371.
9. E. Monro, *Parochial Work* (Parker, Oxford, 1850), pp.17ff.
10. ibid., pp.33ff.
11. ibid., pp.87ff and 120ff.
12. ibid., pp.132ff.
13. ibid., pp.141ff.
14. J.H. Blunt, *Directorium Pastorale: Principles and Practice of Pastoral Work in the Church of England* (Rivingtons, London, 1864).
15. F.D. How, *Bishop Walsham How: A Memoir* (Isbister, London, 1899), pp.92f.
16. Bradlaugh was a leading figure in the Victorian secularist movement.
17. W.W. How, *Lectures on Pastoral Work* (Wells Gardner, Darton, London, 1883), pp.81ff.
18. ibid., pp.101ff.
19. J.G. Lockhart, *Cosmo Gordon Lang* (Hodder and Stoughton, London, 1949).
20. C.G. Lang, *The Opportunity of the Church of England* (London, 1905), p.6.
21. ibid., pp.33ff.
22. ibid., p.9
23. ibid., pp.6ff
24. ibid., p.49.

25. J.P. Norris, *Lectures on Pastoral Theology* (London, 1884).
26. J. M. Wilson, *Six Lectures on Pastoral Theology* (Macmillan, London, 1903).
27. Rogers (1912), op.cit., pp.36 and 175ff.
28. Martin Thornton, *Pastoral Theology: A Reorientation* (SPCK, London, 1958); Michael Ramsey, *The Christian Priest Today* (SPCK, London, 1972). See also Peter Davie, *Pastoral Care and the Parish* (Blackwell, Oxford, 1983).

A Light at Nightfall: The Dissolution of Christendom as an Opportunity for Anglican Renewal

Samuel L. Edwards

That this is an age of dissolution is no new insight. One hears it in the autumnal strains of the music of Sir Edward Elgar and Gustav Mahler as well as in the famous observation by Sir Edward Grey on the eve of the First World War that 'The lights are going out all over Europe, and we shall not see them lit again in our lifetime'. Ireland's William Butler Yeats distilled it in his short poem, 'The Second Coming,' published in 1927, which has become something of an anthem for this age:

> Turning and turning in the widening gyre
> The falcon cannot hear the falconer;
> Things fall apart; the centre cannot hold;
> Mere anarchy is loosed upon the world,
> The blood-dimmed tide is loosed, and everywhere
> The ceremony of innocence is drowned;
> The best lack all conviction, while the worst
> Are full of passionate intensity;
> Surely some revelation is at hand;
> Surely the Second Coming is at hand.[1]

Yeats goes on, of course, to present a vision of a 'rough beast, its hour come round at last' (after 'twenty centuries of stony sleep ... vexed to nightmare by a rocking cradle') which 'slouches towards

Bethlehem to be born'. Although his prophecy has proved accurate, Yeats' foresight is limited: all he can offer is a ground for anxiety without a basis for hope, so his is an oracle accurate but incomplete. He can diagnose, but he has no prescription. He can describe the darkness, but he cannot point us toward the light. It would be unfair to expect this of him: fundamentally, Yeats is a pagan, and the best one can expect from pagans is noble resignation. More can be expected from Christians, and ought to be, for as one who was a lesser poet but a better philosopher than Yeats wrote,

> The men of the East may spell the stars,
> And times and triumphs mark,
> But the men signed of the cross of Christ
> Go gaily in the dark.[2]

However, the age of dissolution in which we live is at the same time an age of convergence and of realignment. We are living through what has become fashionable to call a 'paradigm shift,' when institutions and customary habits of thought and behavior which had been assumed to be permanent are becoming ineffective, irrelevant, even self-destructive. Such things have happened before, of course. One thinks of the period around the fifth century on the continent of Western Europe, or of the departure of the Romans from Britain, of the crisis of the Reformation. Yet, if history teaches us anything, it is that such periods presage the emergence of a new paradigm. It is my intention in this paper briefly to describe that which is passing, to comment on that which seems to be emerging, and to suggest a few ways in which the new paradigm may affect the practice of the church.

The Dissolution of Christendom.

It is important to note that the convergence which has been mentioned, and of which more will be said later, is taking place at precisely the same time as the dissolution of what we may call the *Christendom ecclesiology*, meaning the fundamental assumptions concerning the institutional church and its relationship to the secular world which have been in place since the Constantinian era. The ideal of this relationship is a symphony between church and state, between the sacred and the secular. In a way, this idea looks toward the final harmonization of all things at the fulfillment of history, when Christ 'delivers the kingdom to God the Father after destroying every rule and every authority and power ... that God may be everything to everyone'.[3] However, human nature being what it is, this ideal has sooner or later been corrupted by a secular messianism (explicit or implicit) which forgets both the fact that 'here we have no lasting city,'[4] and the Lord's own injunction not to believe or follow those who come saying, 'Lo, there, or lo, here.'[5]

So far as the faithful maintenance of the Christian faith was concerned, the Christendom model created no major problem, so long as the general assumptions in the surrounding society remained Christian. However, the difficulty with it became progressively more evident as the Western world began to de-christianize in the wake of the Enlightenment. One might suggest that the philosophical roots of the trouble lie in the nominalism of the fourteenth century, which paved the intellectual highway leading to the twin modern plagues of individualism and collectivism through its abandonment of the focus on the being of God in favor of a concentration on his sovereign will. However that may be, at least since the eighteenth century the Western world has been moving away from Christianity through secularism toward profanity. The church in the modern world seems to be moving into a setting which has progressively less in common with its situation in the the post-Constantinian world, in which the Church was first approved, then endorsed, and finally dominated (most of the time) by the *saeculum* than it does with the pre-Constantinian world, when the Church was alternately tolerated and persecuted, but never approved, by a civilization as morally decadent and as intellectually exhausted, as sentimental and as cruel as that of the modern 'First World.'

In the sixteen hundred years that have elapsed since the Edict of Milan, and particularly since the beginning of the modern era, the practical basis of the church has come to be understood more and more in *institutional* terms: churches are seen as deriving their cohesiveness from common institutions with a national, international, or historical basis. At the same time, at least among Anglicans and other mainstream Protestants (which in the United States and in much of the 'First World' somewhat paradoxically includes elements within the Roman Catholic Church) less and less emphasis has been placed on common faith and order as the essential element binding Christians together. The spread of secularism and liberal democratic idealism have contributed materially both to this de-emphasis on orthodox doctrine and to the consequent disintegration of the ordinal and confessional elements of ecclesiastical practice. As a result, the institutions of the Church (which are separable from her order and dependent for their legitimacy on their adherence to that order) are too often found on the wrong side of the lines in the cultural war which presently convulses Western society.

What has happened to the Anglican Communion over the last two decades is a clear example of what is coming about as a consequence of this disintegration. With the ordination of women, we now have an admittedly provisional (and therefore dubious) form of ordained ministry in several provinces which cannot function in other provinces. Some of the newer proposed and official prayer books (one thinks immediately of the New Zealand book) set forth sacramental and dogmatic theologies with scant resemblance to classical Anglican teaching. In light of this, it would seem that the basis of communion for Anglicans in effect has been reduced to the invitation list for the Lambeth Conference. Indeed, one might be forgiven for asking whether the term 'Anglican Communion' is still meaningful, when the fundamental conditions for sacramental communion between churches—namely, common faith and a mutually recognized ministry—no longer exist within it. The Anglican Communion may well have become an Association of the Descendants of the English Reformation, having the same basic standard for membership as a genealogical society in which legitimate descent from the ancestral group rather than fidelity to its principles is the determinative qualification.

Church Order and Church Institutions

Since much of what has been said so far and much of what follows depends on the contention that there is a distinction between the institutions *in* the Church and the order *of* the Church, it is now appropriate to briefly define the distinction. Far from being anything new, these distinctions are clearly present in the Thirty-Nine Articles of Religion and ultimately are drawn out of Scripture itself.

The order *of* the Church consists of those basic elements of her life given her by her Lord which are indispensable to her faithful witness to the world. These elements are the Holy Scriptures, the two Dominical Sacraments, the Historic Creeds, and the Apostolic Ministry. These are 'givens': the Church is not allowed to change them in any substantial way and the Christian mission is to bring the gospel to all people through their use.

The institutions *in* the Church, on the other hand, are those things which are set up by the members of the Church for the purpose of forwarding the gospel most efficiently. They can change and, from time to time, should be changed so that they continue to help and not to hinder the Church's mission.

Church order and church institutions are always tied up together, but it is not that difficult to distinguish them. One example from each category should suffice: the institutional church may not add to, take away from, or rewrite Holy Scripture by excision, supplementation, or dishonest re-translation, but it may organize it into lectionaries for public reading (so long as these do not gut or alter the whole message of Scripture through a tendentious selectiveness). It may not permit baptism with rose petals in the name of the Creator, Redeemer, and Sanctifier instead of baptism with water in the name of the Father and of the Son and of the Holy Spirit, but it may issue orders of service for the administration of Holy Baptism. It may not strike any element from the creeds, but it may issue explanations of the creeds, such as catechisms, so long as these do not muddle or contradict what the creeds plainly say. It may not abolish the episcopate in the succession of the Apostles' teaching and fellowship, but it may alter the form in which it is continued and exercised, so long as the alteration does not contradict scriptural standards. In sum, then, we may not change the Church's order, but we may change her institutions to enable her to fulfill her mission, so long as the institutional change proposed does not in fact violate that basic order.

Convergence and Realignment

From the same process that produces vinegar, wine may issue, and the forces that convulse the earth may at the same time expose a vein of precious metal. When the God who acts in history permits an old order to pass away, we may be sure that the new is already emerging beneath it. Many observers of different schools, possessed of different agendas, have commented upon the phenomenon that, since the old confessional and denominational lines no longer seem to be as significant as they once did, many within those historic groupings have been finding a new commonality of vision and purpose. Graham Leonard, who prior to his reception into the Roman Communion was a notable exponent of this view, referred to the phenomenon as a 'massive realignment' which is 'likely to acquire the dimensions of a second Reformation'[6] and which is taking place across and with scant regard to the old denominational lines between those who affirm the given-ness of the catholic and apostolic faith and those who wish, as the phrase goes, to 'earth' Christianity in this present world. The old denominationalism appears to be on its way out, and with it the late-comer Anglo-American phenomenon known as 'Anglicanism'.[7] One can find in this a cause for rejoicing, and for this reason when someone asks the question, 'Does Anglicanism have a future?' one may respond to it by saying, 'I certainly hope not. Once we are rid of it, perhaps we can get down to the business of recovering the Anglican way of being a reformed catholic Christian'. One aspect of such a recovery surely would be a practical reappropriation of the oft-quoted observation of Archbishop Fisher that we Anglicans have no faith of our own.

It is important to realize that this convergence and realignment has a dual nature: there is a convergence of the orthodox and a convergence of the heterodox; there is a godly convergence and an ungodly convergence. This is always a feature of the confrontation with Christ, as we can see from the New Testament: To take but two examples, there is a convergence *in* Christ between Jew and Gentile, such as that between Peter and Cornelius; but there is also a convergence *against* Christ between Jew and Gentile, such as that between Herod and Pilate. Given such a dynamic, it probably should not be as surprising as it usually is to see, for instance, Southern Baptists making common cause and covenant with Roman Catholics, Roman nuns making common cause with Anglican feminists, and pentecostal churches seeking to receive the gift of apostolic ministry. Indeed, our time is one of opportunity, but as often as not, opportunity brings confusion with it.

For us, who are called of God to serve him in this time, (to borrow Lincoln's words), 'the dogmas of the quiet past are inadequate to the stormy present. The occasion is piled high with difficulty, and we must rise with the occasion ... [W]e must think anew and act anew. We must disenthrall ourselves...'[8]

Now, from what attitudes and assumptions must Anglicans be disenthralled, and (more positively) what renewed attitudes and assumptions must Anglicans adopt if we are to rise with the occasion, if we are to faithfully serve God in the Great Convergence? Reform is needed in at least three main areas: pastoral practice, the model of the episcopate, and the approach to Christian unity.

Reform in Pastoral Practice

One assumption that needs to be challenged and changed is the idea that valid orders and liturgical skill can substitute for orthodox teaching and pastoral commitment. It may well be that the average churchman does not really care very much either about our ecclesiastical pedigree or about how elegant a figure the clergyman cuts at the altar.

What, then, does the churchman want of his church and her pastors? He wants what penitent sinners in every generation have wanted: he wants the proclamation in power and integrity—in Word as well as in Sacrament—of his heritage in Christ, which is an eternal Gospel which convicts him of sin, gives him a living hope that through trust in the merits of Christ he can be freed of it, and assures him that through the indwelling Spirit of God he—even he—can become holy. He wants forms of worship which help him appropriate that, behind which the first question asked was not, 'is this more like the early Roman rite of Hippolytus?' or 'is the language here inclusive?' but 'does this adequately show forth the infinite and intimate majesty, the exalted and exalting humility, and the sweet and severe compassion of the Father, and of the Son, and of the Holy Spirit?' Of equal importance, he wants ready access to a caring and understanding pastor who has both the time and the inclination to 'get personal' on how his every-day life relates to the gospel message.

Practically speaking, if a churchman is serious about his pilgrim-age Godward and leaves the Anglican Church because he can find no help in it, he is more likely to go to a Bible Church in search of evan-gelical truth than he is to become Roman Catholic or Eastern Orthodox in search of institutional security. Only as the pastors of the Church give attention to this can they authenticate their claim to be in the succession of the apostles. For the churchman, apostolic is as apostolic teaches, and holy is as holy lives. For him, our ministry is not validated by our pedigree; our pedigree is validated by our fidelity. If the pastors are not faithful, the validity of their orders only serves to condemn them before God and humanity.

Reform in the Model of the Episcopate

Another assumption that needs to be challenged in light both of the collapse of Christendom and of the Great Convergence is the idea that fixed institutional and geographical elements are central to the life of the Church. With regard to the episcopate, we must give serious thought to its reformation in light of the aforementioned dissolution of the Christendom ecclesiology. That ecclesiology, originating as a result of imperial establishment and papal modifications thereof, supported a model of episcopal ministry which itself took on an impe-rial character, with the bishop seen as the ruler of all Christians within a defined territory—a model which is, I believe, significantly differ-ent from that which obtained in the pre-Constantinian age. Habits of practice and thought continued that model beyond the collapse of the societal structures which supported it, but its inadequacy to the stormy present has become both increasingly apparent and embarrassing. It has become somewhat surreal—rather like a Dali painting of a castle perched on a rock, which itself is suspended in mid-air with no visible means of support.

It must be pointed out that an attempt (albeit a largely unconscious one) to supply the obvious need for a new model of the episcopate has been made in the West: there has been an attempt to move from an imperial into what I would call a managerial model of the episcopate. This is particularly evident in the United States, though it is by no means confined within their borders, as we can see from recent proposals concerning performance reviews and the abolition of the parson's freehold in England. The managerial model has this to be said for it: it is very efficient at accomplishing the goals it sets. However, it appears to have no capacity for evaluating the worthiness of these goals. The attempt to substitute the managerial for the imperial episcopate has failed because (being based as it is on worldly and not on scriptural ideas) the managerial model does nothing to address the chief need in today's (or any day's) episcopate, which is the maintenance of apostolic faith and order. In fact, it has actually made the problem worse through its inherent tendency to take the path of least resistance to secularity and profanity. Indeed, in this case, our former state is worse than the previous one: the old demon of prelaticism, having been expelled, has returned and brought a management team with him. And one doubts whether exchanging the style of Pius the Ninth for that of H. Ross Perot is really much of an improvement.

Now, this call for a reformation of the character of the episcopate is not an exercise in rootless revolution. Change in the concept of this essential ministry has happened before: Dom Gregory Dix, in his monograph on *Jurisdiction in the Early Church: Episcopal and Papal*,[9] points out that the sudden legitimization of the Church, followed quickly by its civil establishment, led rapidly to a shift in the view of the episcopate: the bishop came to be seen less as the teacher of a people than as the ruler of a territory. In other words, a model of the episcopate that could be described as paterfamilial and pastoral was exchanged for one that was fundamentally monarchical and imperial. In the mind of the average person, and in that of the average bishop, the bishop went from being 'Father' to being 'my Lord Bishop'.

The Reformation only inadequately addressed the problem. On the continent, the Reformers (save in Sweden) either threw out the episcopate altogether or (as did Calvin) redefined it. In England, while a desire for something like the ancient paterfamilial model was expressed (especially in the Ordinal) and even on occasion embodied (one thinks of men such as Latimer and Ridley), the medieval monarchical model remained in force.

What I would commend is filling the void left by the circumstan-
tially-enforced collapse of the old imperial view of the episcopate by
an intentional recapture of the pre-Constantinian paterfamilial model.
This will necessarily parallel the replacement of mainly institutional
and political concepts of the Church herself with an organic and familial model.

This new model, or renewed model, has distinct advantages. Like
the pre-Constantinian concept, it is flexible and resilient. It sets the
bishop within the context of a worshiping community without making
him a mere functionary. It works well with an important ecclesiological principle (never entirely repudiated and having recent examples
in the United States, New Zealand, and Southern Africa), which is
that jurisdiction over peoples is antecedent to jurisdiction over terri-
tories. It provides the potential for an acceptable settlement of many
of our present difficulties within the Anglican Communion—a potential which may well be more capable of realization than was previously
the case, now that our Communion is less a Communion and more
an association of churches with a common root in this soil. Whether
this potential in fact will be realized is another question.

This potential for settlement is well described by Dr Jeffrey
Steenson, who writes of our current Anglican situation that

> Usually a mood of mutuality and respect prevails in ecumenical
> relations. But within our own communion it is a different matter
> entirely. The territorial *episcopē* is being used to obliterate our clas-
> sical Anglican convictions. [The ESA's] parallel province proposal
> gets rejected out of hand because the Anglican bishops at Lambeth
> don't like the idea of parallel episcopal jurisdiction: 'Within his
> diocese, the bishop is the focus of unity. The ideal for Anglicans
> as for many other Christians is that there should be one bishop in
> each place' [*Ecumenical Relations* 40 (1988)].
>
> However, Dr [Allan] Brent [a patristics scholar and Senior
> Lecturer in History at Australia's University of North Queensland]
> has suggested that this territorial *episcopē* is a relatively recent devel-
> opment in church history. He argues that it is closely related to the
> rise of the modern nation-state, in which sovereignty is conceived in
> terms of jurisdiction over territory. Originally, however, jurisdiction
> was principally over people, and as such it was the reflection of a
> common cultural and ethnic identity that served to unite a people. Dr
> Brent argues that in our post-industrial multi-cultural world this
> cultural model of social organization is the more viable. Our
> advances in transportation and communication have made the territo-
> rial model something of an anachronism.

This idea has real possibilities for resolving the dilemma Anglicans everywhere are facing about reconciling two vastly different theological systems, the traditional and the modernist. What if we were to base episcopal jurisdiction not on the arbitrary divisions of geography but on the more natural distinctions of theological identity? Or to put it another way, what if the Episcopal Church were to become an ecumenical city, where its various communities would preserve their individual distinctiveness, including their representative forms of ordained ministry.[10]

One great advantage to the a recovery of a truly paterfamilial episcopate and of the New Testament understanding of the Church as the family of God is that it would give all shades of Anglicans (including the traditional variety) an equal footing in the religious free market. Of course, this is precisely the feature that makes such a solution so unappealing to the present corporatist and modernist power-structure of the Episcopal Church. (One has to admit that it would probably be an equally unappealing solution to a corporatist and conservative power-structure.) By and large, the distaste for the notion of a parallel province (or, following Dr Brent, 'cultural episcopates') is not rooted in a conscious and intellectually coherent conviction about the nature of the Church, however much it may appeal to ecclesiological categories. The resistance appears instead to come from a subliminal perception that to allow evangelical catholics and catholic evangelicals a distinct and sustainable identity within the Episcopal Church would deprive the corporatists and modernists both of their monopoly on defining Anglican Christianity (the external challenge to which, incidentally, is why they abhor the existence of the so-called Continuing Churches) and eventually, perhaps, of the spiritual and material resources which they may be incapable of generating for themselves.

Perhaps the most important aspect of the recovery of this earlier model of the episcopate is its emphasis that the *magisterium* of the episcopate is based entirely upon orthodoxy: where such an emphasis is present, it tends to foster a situation in which the teacher is seen as leader, but the people are following the teaching, not the teacher. This is the reason why the pessimism of some concerning authority within the Anglican Way is in error. The *magisterium* will reappear when institutional leaders once again teach right doctrine.

The effecting of this change of model for the episcopate will be difficult, but not so difficult as one might think. The reason for this is that it accords with what the ordinary churchman wants in a bishop: a Father-in-God who will define Christian identity by proclaiming the truth, keeping godly order in the household, encouraging and enabling the pastors under him to be pastors and teachers of the truth, and showing a principled and courteous concern for all the members of God's family.

Reform in the Approach to Unity

There seems to be an interior impetus toward unity and order which develops among Christians when their priority is not denominational aggrandizement but obedience to the Word of God. This accounts for the fact that other Christians very often do 'get it right' without having access to our tradition's attitudes and institutional customs. For instance, there is an increasing recognition among certain evangelical and pentecostal Christians of a need for rootedness in historic Christianity, resulting in the Evangelical Orthodox phenomenon, in the recent admission of an entire independent pentecostal congregation into the Diocese of Georgia, in the reported desire of certain English pentecostal groups to come into full membership in the Church of England, in enquiries to the same effect which have borne fruit in the Episcopal Missionary Church, and in the phenomenal growth of the Charismatic Episcopal Church. Sometimes the initial reaction of traditional Anglicans toward such moves has been not unlike that of their corporatist and modernist opponents: to them, it is strange and unsettling, falling as it does outside the familiar patterns in which they understand themselves and others ecclesiastically. This is regrettable, for what really is going on when such a thing happens is an instance of the Great Convergence.

It would be well to appropriate the spirit which moved the American Anglican priest William Augustus Muhlenberg to make his famous 'Memorial' to the General Convention of 1853. In this document, it was proposed that, in the interests of the extension of the gospel and of Christian unity, the gift of the apostolic ministry be extended to men and congregations of sound faith who 'could not bring themselves to conform in all particulars to our prescriptions and customs'.[11] Full consideration of this truly prophetic proposal was interrupted by the outbreak of the War for Southern Independence, and though it was very influential in laying the groundwork for what became the Chicago/Lambeth Quadrilateral, its promise, like that of the English Reformation itself, has yet fully to be worked out. Now that the Christendom idea – and the denominationalism which was its adaptation to the Reformation/Counter-reformation – is dissolving and now that convergence and realignment are underway, the opportunity to work out its promise is now upon us.

If classical Anglicans are to rise to this occasion, then they must be fully willing to make common cause with those who share their commitments to apostolic faith and order, even when their commitment to the order part of the equation is still only embryonic, and to leave it to God to see to its maturation by his own means. Obviously, this would include both those evangelical protestant groups who are increasingly discovering their roots in the sub-apostolic Church, and those in the 'Continuing Anglican' movement who are too often subjected to scornful stonethrowing on the part of those who dwell in the glass house of 'official Anglicanism.'

How will this new ecumenism go down with the typical churchman? Better than most clergy types might think to begin with. It is often, and correctly, perceived (and sometimes bemoaned) that the average lay person is very attached to his denominational identity. However, what often escapes the notice of the clergy is that this attachment is very largely positive ('I like being an Anglican') and only negligibly negative ('I thank thee, Lord, that I am not as other Christians – Baptists, Methodists, Presbyterians, Lutherans, Roman Catholics'). One might argue that the reason for this lacuna in clerical observation has to do with the clergy's closer involvement with and investment in the institutional church and in the professional tendency to promote one's own way of doing things. The layman, however, is not in the position of receiving his daily bread from the hand of the institutional church, and while he would no doubt be glad to see his Christian friends be Anglicans, he sees them primarily as fellow soldiers of Christ's army serving in different regiments. The typical churchman is not likely to be offended by other Christians receiving Communion in his parish church, nor will he be too proud to receive instruction from the leaders of other Christian bodies, nor will he object to working with and serving under them in projects directed toward the accomplishment of common Christian objectives.

A Cautionary Conclusion

Having said all this, it must also be said that none of this needed reform will take place overnight. There is a trap lurking for traditional Christians in the insistence that reform be fully accomplished immediately, if not sooner, or else. We have seen the damage done to the family of God by our modernist opponents' insistence on rapid change, and we must not suppose that our being similarly implacable will produce no harm. It were well that we remember that the tested stone, the precious cornerstone of the sure foundation which the Lord lays is inscribed, 'He who believes will not be in haste'.[12] Undue haste is a sign of defective faith, of a loss of perspective concerning Whose Church this is and Who, therefore, is in charge of the working out of the present distress.

We can take a lesson about what *not* to do from English church history. We all are familiar with the damage done to the Church of England by the Puritan party with its insistence on rapid remaking of the church. What we are not so likely to appreciate is the damage done to the Church of England as a consequence of the Restoration policy of church and Parliament which, while rightly asserting the need for the ministers of the national church to receive episcopal ordination, wrongly caused the rapid ejection from their livings even of non-conformists who were good pastors without consideration for the effect of such action on the laity. One might fairly speculate that the pursuance of the same objective by a method of attrition and replacement with episcopally-ordained men would have given less grounds for the growth of both dissent and unbelief in England during that period and beyond.

Those who are naturally attracted by the examples of Elijah defeating the prophets of Ba'al on Mount Carmel and of Jesus cleansing the Temple with a whip of cords will do well if we remember that our Lord himself once healed a blind man by stages.[13] It is significant that this passage immediately follows one in which Jesus upbraids his disciples for their spiritual blindness to his identity and immediately precedes the account of the confession at Caesarea Philippi. It took *them* time to get it right, in spite of the sign of the loaves: it scarcely seems realistic to expect that all Jesus' disciples in this generation will get it right instantaneously. The healing of our present distress in faith and order may have to take place by stages as well. Anyone who has been a parish priest knows that patience, deliberation, and persuasion provide a better method of making desirable changes in all but the most extreme cases. He who believes and who therefore is not in haste can put up with a lot, provided he is clear on what God wants to accomplish for the benefit of his Church through his ministry. And for each of us who are privileged to minister in this era of convergence, what God wishes to accomplish through our ministry is the fulfillment of our Lord's high priestly prayer that all those who believe on his Name become perfectly one in his Truth that the world may believe that he is the Way by which it may enter into the Life of the Father, and of the Son, and of the Holy Ghost, to Whose Triune Majesty be all honor and glory, now and for ever.

Notes

1. W. B. Yeats, 'The Second Coming,' H. Spencer, W. E. Houghton, H. Barrows, eds., *British Literature: Blake to the Present Day*, 2nd edn., (D. C. Heath and Company, Lexington, Massachusetts, 1963), p.904.
2. G. K. Chesterton, 'The Ballad of the White Horse,' *The Collected Poems of G. K. Chesterton* (Dodd, Mead, & Company, New York, 1980), p. 216.
3. 1 Cor. 15.24, 28. [All biblical quotations are from the Revised Standard Version.]
4. Hebrews 13.14.
5. Luke 17.23.
6. A. D. Davies, general ed., *The Episcopal Synod of America: Speeches, Sermons, Documents and Pictures from the Founding Meeting* (Morehouse Publishing, Wilton, Connecticut, 1990), pp. 53f.
7. It is worth noting that the term 'Anglicanism' itself is relatively new word: its first recorded appearance in English, according to the *Oxford English Dictionary*, is in a collection of works by Charles Kingsley published in 1846.
8. Quoted by S. Foote, *The Civil War, A Narrative: Fort Sumter to Perryville* (Vintage Books, New York, 1958), p. 810.
9. Dom Gregory Dix, *Jurisdiction in the Early Church: Episcopal and Papal* (Church Literature Association, London, 1975). Note especially Chapter III.
10. J. N. Steenson, 'Province X Revisited,' a presentation to the Legislative Body of the Episcopal Synod of America at Chicago, Illinois, 19 April 1991.
11. S. E. Ahlstrom, *A Religious History of the American People* (Yale University Press, New Haven and London, 1972), p. 630.
12. Isa. 28.16.
13. cf. Mark 8.22ff.